The Analyst:

THERE IS A BOUNTY ON MY HEAD

DR. MADALINA DAY

NEW BEGINNINGS THERAPY

The Analyst: *There is a bounty on my head*

The Analyst: *There is a bounty on my head*

For my son

The Analyst: *There is a bounty on my head*

The Analyst: *There is a bounty on my head*

Contents:

The Analyst: *There is a bounty on my head*

Introduction: Summary and terminology/perspectives

"...The identifications and tendencies belonging to an analyst's personal experiences and personal development which provide the positive setting for his analytic work and make his work different in quality from that of any other analyst.... I distinguish the truly objective counter-transference, or if this is difficult, the analyst's love and hate in reaction to the actual personality and behaviour of the patient, based on objective observation. I suggest that if an analyst is to analyse psychotics or anti-socials he must be able to be so thoroughly aware of the counter-transference that he can sort out and study his <u>objective reactions</u> to the patient. These will include hate. Counter-transference phenomena will at times be the important things in the analysis. " (Winnicott, 1949,p.69)

There are a total of 11 chapters in this text, an analytical textbook. Cases presented in chapters 1 to 10 are real patients in psychoanalysis over a period of ten years across three decades.

The subject text is described:

An analytic read focussed on several settings of psychoanalytic practice. This text presents a cumulative of 19 case studies from Psychoanalysis practice and research. In its entirety, narratives would be of help to any human being with an interest in self-comprehension, and their capacity to endure previously never encountered challenges. Dr. Madalina Day is the analyst in text with "there is a bounty on my head" referencing an acute threat that Dr. Day had EXPERIENCED from various levels of the UK Government over the past decades, culminating with an attempt to discredit her professionally. Instead, the writing communicates the real elephant in the room and how, in analytical therapy, the most likely outcome is "falling on your own sword" when harm and ethical violence are aimed as responses to an analyst (Dr. Day). The Analyst details such an uncalculated attack from: the National Health Services (NHS) in the UK, and the British Association for Counselling and Psychotherapy (BACP) pointing at Dr. Madalina Day. This lecture is an ultimate view on how to recognise deflection and poverty of principles, now explicitly published by Dr. Day, volume I of the Analyst, as a guide tour for both the NHS and the BACP. Hope it helps IT.

The Analyst: *There is a bounty on my head*

Chapter 1: There is always another way

Not long after terminating an honorary contract (2014-2020/2023) at one of the largest NHS Trust in England, Croydon Health Services NHS Trust, I was faced with a difficult and complex dilemma, proposed to I by actions prompted by former honorary contract and its clients: **what do I do next**?

Before I explain, in full, that event question, a recap of why I offered my services to an NHS Trust psychotherapy/counselling service for the NHS staff, is now long overdue. I could say that it was simply by chance, but I know better than that.

Sometime in 2013, I was completing year 3 out of 5 of a dual BSc degree (my 5th undergraduate and postgraduate) on Psychodynamic and Cognitive Behavioural Therapy (CBT) at Birkbeck, University of London and, concurrently, I was updating my knowledge of British Psychological Society (BPS) Postgraduate Diploma in Psychology for registration with the BPS at Metropolitan University, London. At that time, I was a single mum since 2009, but in truth, I felt single quite immediately after the birth of my son in 2004. As financial means, I was also receiving a miserable allocation after all marital assets were sold, disparaged by my ex and eventually parted with less than 20% on my side and my son's side. I did not have a strong legal team representing my interests and/or my son's interests, and to some extent that was entirely my fault. All pre-divorce events, felt like a tsunami on my being, and for a period of several years, as a matter of fact, things felt devastating. Nevertheless, my and my son's situation are no particularly exceptional, except if assessed under Equality Act 2010 and discrimination legislation. Most extraordinary aspects were also my main motivation: that of looking into the future, ensuring that I will not give up, no matter what. Chief determination was my self-belief. Armoured with such priority, I continued learning, practicing analysis, writing (my volume of poems is dated from before 2010, and was published in 2021, now in bilingual edition), and do outreach community work - some as employment, some voluntary, and some honorary employment i.e. psychotherapy to the NHS staff.

For that latter so called honour, sometime in autumn/winter 2014 and during a final year 4/5 of a programme at Birkbeck, University of London, I completed academic research modules for the BPS accredited Postgraduate Diploma in Psychology. I made an active choice to continue on with psychoanalysis and psychotherapy, alongside psychology as mainstream profession and already an education of my second university degree.

Both post/ and under/graduate studies were self-financed – always, and being number 4th and 5th of my educational experience, intended as a reminder of who I am. At that same time, I started my thesis for one PhD programme – all self-financed through my private practice, always called as advancing my understanding in psychoanalysis at postgraduate level. At any rate, and at that moment in time, learning, in principle, was a form of self-validation and somehow extraordinary after my marriage was terminated. Potentially, it can be asserted that my latter years of studying formed part of a wanting to overcome a perceived post-marital disaster. My divorce did not feel like a failure at the time of happening, it felt like a liberation, removing the chains of what, at times, felt like servitude with contrasting values deeply embedded in the institution of marriage. What it was not realised at the time of divorce, was that I was also removing myself and my son from financial security of life as it was known to us both up to that point in time. More importantly, I was dislocating chains of servitude at the price of my son and I being at risk for life and unsafe shelter in the UK. In aiming for a continuation of my practice in the UK and worldwide, envisaged past my retirement years, I was hoping to balance out and replace such a perceived risk, potentially replenish our situation in good time. I was wrong in my expectations, and my hopes that same system that would take everything from me and my son, will in any forthcoming way, allow me to rebuild my life in my own terms, especially when I was always going to call it out for what I see it as a faulty system and structure.

When I started clinical client work at the NHS (National Health Service) Trust in 2014/2015, I had my private practice going for decades, and my services in analysis and psychotherapy were active in other four settings. None of my professional duties were a requirement for the undergraduate degree at Birkbeck, with one exception of an 100 hours proof of psychoanalysis performed in 24 months future period. I, instead, completed that requirement within the first three weeks of course commencing in 2012. And yet, when Angela Armstrong, head therapist lead at Croydon Health Services NHS Trust, offered me an interview and honorary job, I felt intrigued. I questioned the place' potential because the NHS's offer was from within an unique service in the NHS, at least at that time 2014/2015. The NHS, as a corporation, has a very contested history, and when I analysed the NHS, both through their staff and as an organisation, my analysis did not and will not ever bring about full on positive reflections. I was clearly aware that there are challenges beyond belief, and I conceptualised the NHS based on, or rather its foundations, at a continuum ***at war*** principle of existence. "At war", and mainly internally, caused by understaffing, lack of appropriate and efficient infrastructure, and funding.

Staff shortages and implicit risk are crucially perpetuating a dis-service to the NHS itself, and to the UK population at large. The NHS's image of a caring and dedicated public service free at point of use, which the UK public are referring to and hold tight when continuing to access it, is a myth and it simply doesn't exist. The NHS as a good fairy public service is an ideal, that is my clinical opinion and based on evidence: a 74 years old myth that aims to work like a placebo effect for all, whereas in reality manages 28% risk on mortality of all its cases, and that as a positive outcome. In reality, and reality is my chief concern, the NHS is in crumble, pieces, fragments of what it aims to be, and the very agents achieving such a desolate reality are employees of the NHS in its majority – not honorary or volunteering. Paid employees, dissatisfied and blind to their own harming the NHS. Perhaps one day, myth and reality may be achieved, but as it stands, years of 2023/2024/2025/2026 and 2027, the UK will experience an NHS that is 89% of mortality rates, mainly or merely owed to its own standards of practice with its staff absolutely out of reach with health manifestations of the UK public. No parameters of analysis can be improved, except if entire NHS ceases to exist with immediate effect. Mortality rates, majorly due to malpractice in the NHS (inferred by staff shortages and underfunding) are an average of 69% to 79% some reported some hidden in very statistics provided by various NHS reports - that is the risk in 2023, likely to continue for next 5 years on a higher per units and rate. I can give you statistics, I just did. One healthy remark would be that I am wrong and/or disgruntled. Unfortunately, to such thoughts, I can tell you that I have 99.9% precision on my scientific/statistical observations.

For six years, I've observed and actively consulted in the NHS, and even if honorary, I could feel, or rather sense its dying pulse. Change can still happen and potentially new wave of staff strikes, or Government promises, or opposition party pledges for next election, might decrease mortality rates by 1% to 5% at its most hopeful criteria of outcome. The NHS needs full reform and such change in outcomes requires a minimum of ten years of drastic changes including outstanding investment in infrastructure. If the NHS has 100 billion£ investment and 789 new hospitals build and staffed within the next 24 months, then a reverse of current catastrophic outcomes have a chance of turning the tide. Is there any current talk of such investment by current Government and/or pledges from the opposition party?

Here is reform pledge simplified, specifically on major points:

1.Staff shortages;

2. Review of all organisational policies, particularly concerning public safety and whistleblowing policies;

3. A new independent body supervising the NHS processing serious incidents concerning public safety; a Permanent Independent Commission (PIC);

What I am reiterating above are not new statistics/ideas, on the contrary, I have tried, and in the best possible ways, through my practice, alerting the NHS and its clinical staff to all such views - all continuous during my honorary contract and post-honorary contract. Outcomes are also published via books and blogs. The NHS and I are not, by all means, in good terms, in fact, it can be decisively stated that there are no terms, except an outstanding invoice at one NHS Trust' finance department and legal department for daring to address me on three consecutive instances after my termination of my relationship with that Trust.

Included at end of chapter are emails with request for payment that was considered harassment on my part, whereas in very fact, I was treated as a servant and ultimately the NHS Trust prompted and completed a series of attacks on my professional life continuously and incessantly since 2021.

I guess that was the price to pay for my services to the NHS for analysing and providing honorary services under a honorary contract of employment. Sometime in 2021, I was contacted by another NHS Trust in conjunction to an invoice that I paid personally for a postgraduate course accessed for specialism of CBT (cognitive behavioural therapy), mainly because my client work had increased to seven (7) fold, and I was also appointed to supply assessments and take on the whole NHS psychotherapeutic service when Emma Ulysses, the lead therapist, was on holiday. Assessments were not a problem, as I always conducted my own assessments, but the NHS Trust and I, disagreed on several issues, including prescription of number of therapeutic sessions and modality of therapy offered to its employees. Six sessions was what was prescribed in majority of cases, and I strongly, thoroughly disagreed. For 24 months, I thought that there was a clear agreement that I will extend and reformulate assessments. In some cases, six sessions was simply not enough. None of the CBT protocols work on six sessions – it does nothing, there is no measurable data to confirm that six sessions could be used in statistics or any qualitative way for real affect changes. I simply thought that changes to previous policies can be implemented and equally, I'd hoped, that maybe a refresher training on my part can achieve success with 12 sessions, and only on specific cases. It is not that I did not trust my training, but training must be aligned to both my modality of practice – CBT, and NICE's (National Institute for Care and Excellence) guidelines. The NICE's guidelines are what I was having difficulty with when processing six sessions per patient/case, because scientifically and statistically speaking, that was what it was offered as a service in my practice. There are no CBT protocols prescribing six CBT sessions treatment in NICE's guidelines, and, on average, number of sessions in all protocols totals minimum 38 sessions. Can 6 therapeutic sessions for one specific patient/case be done? Yes, it can, but do not call it "CBT", it can be named something else. Do you see what I mean? My practice could not be the exception. The exception had to be referenced to the client work, and client work and services were not synchronised to my ethical guidelines. My ethical guidelines are also clinical guidelines, and always based on three main principles:

1.   My judgment;
2.   Evidence based studies/research;
3.   Evidence from within the service and clients;

I was not working with three clinical legs, in a manner of speaking, when practicing CBT in six sessions – I was working with two and an amputated one. The evidence-based from NICE's guidelines was the amputated one. Why amputated? Because I could not chase after my initial contract and stipulations. In 2017, Angela Armstrong, lead counsellor retired and when she did, another 4 of my colleagues and honorary appointments resigned within 6 to 12 months. Within the therapy service I had no allies, and in reference to the NHS Trust they were all clients including the Occupational Head Service who supposedly was secondary boss – but I knew better, I had no boss and barely any clinical guidance from within the service. I was never invited to any meetings of the NHS Trust and all reports compiled by the NHS Trust I would access through my own work and what was clearly available to all. Emma would take all my input for clinical excellence and improvements and would introduce it in her own service guidance and assessments. I am talking about ways of clinical assessments, type of assessments, and evidence-based guidance. Did I find that challenging or obtuse? How could I? I was happy, because I thought the service is progressing, but in fact it was not ever developing, it was only saving the NHS Trust serious money with my minimum unpaid 20 hours work a week for years. The evidence-based type of assessments and questionnaires that I introduced to the service, helped many of the staff at the Trust, and that was my only focus throughout my honorary contract. I had a very good relationship with the admin staff working in the OH, as in the last two to three years of my honorary appointment, I was offered an office in the Occupational Health building. At first that change felt less isolating as a practice, but in terms of clinical guidance and meaningful discussions as to how the service was operating, I was not an active participant nominally, except everything I did was exactly that. Perhaps, and in retrospective, it really felt less and less like a professionally growing environment, but by the nature of my work it did not feel in any way difficult in that respect. The training that I enrolled on sometime 2017/2018 was guaranteed by the NHS Trust with Iain Dockerty (Occupational Health Head) putting forward an application for funding prior to course commencing sometime in January 2017. After four/five months and when I already completed first couple of terms, Iain told me that my application for funding was rejected on basis of my CBT practice not actually being seen as a need by the NHS Trust Learning Development Team. By then, I had worked for the NHS Trust for over four years, indeed providing exactly CBT therapeutic modality amongst analysis and psychodynamic psychotherapy and counselling. Eventually, I paid for that part of the course and withdrew from the rest of the year. I did not feel disappointed. I felt bewildered by Iain's and Emma's actions. It was clearly there, black and white, in the application, Iain would indicate that I am saving the trust thousands and thousands a pounds a year by being a band 7/8 clinical staff honorary and yet, the Trust making an allowance for training of a few thousands of pounds was deemed unworthy. Equally clear and also black and white that in my thousands of my weekly reports of my CBT practice and client work, I would detail how CBT can offer such a relief and practical tools of self-help to the NHS staff that would access the service. It is also fair to say that for the first few months of the training, it did not feel like I truly needed it in terms of clinical experience and protocols presented during the weekly training. It was, academically speaking, a repetition of my previous degree on CBT as a modality of practice. I guess that thought erased possibility of feeling in any measure undignified, but what I strongly felt, since my starting clinical work at that NHS Trust, was that the NHS Trust felt that their staff do not deserve better access to specialist services. I flipped that event into thinking that my training was sufficient as it were, and that was the end of it. Except it was not the end of it, because I had to pay back invoices for first terms of the course from my own income as I was already doing with everything else related to costs of my practice at the NHS Trust. Invoices were paid and when three years later, I terminated my practice at Croydon Health Services NHS Trust, I thought everything about my work at that NHS Trust was left behind and in good order. The only items that I still had related to my office there, few months after terminating my honorary appointment, were two books from the University Hospital postgraduate library where I was located. I sent the books off with a note to Emma sometime in January 2021.

I do not feel grateful to that service practice from within the NHS, I do not feel that it had developed me professionally in any sense, I recognise that I developed the service and helped numerous individuals like a pyramid that the NHS staff in turn were able to continue their work, provide security to their families and public patients. Do I feel grateful about that? No, I do not: it was my job, this is what I do. In fairness, how could I feel grateful or think on with fondness towards the NHS Trust and its staff, given the conduct and clear attitude from Emma Ulysses and Iain Dockerty towards I as a professional during the appointment and post-contract? I would simply be disingenuous to suggest that my work in that NHS Trust can be aligned to what majorly contributed to my professional development during same period of time. I, myself and alone, professionally, contributed to my professional advancement and I paid very dearly for it – not only financially, but also emotionally. Psychologically, not so much. My other simultaneous places of practice during same exact six years are sufficiently satisfactory as places of work and development overall. Many other aspects, more personal, are on recall for same period of time and are about my existent support from my family, friends and my client's work clinically developing in great pathways, not specifically services of practice. It is simply in the nature of the work that I do and how I do my work. As to why I would not be thankful to an NHS Trust that regarded my six year term as servant work, it is owed to Croydon Health Services NHS Trust in England that decided to send me a thank you note in the form of a critical failure of human cognisance conveyed in both Emma Ulysses and Iain Dockerty's allegations of breach of data etc. to another failure of a corporation: the British Association for Counselling and Psychotherapy. (BACP). It cannot be more extravagantly and idiotically comic, it simply must be concluded that imbeciles such as Emma Ulysses and Iain Docherty are also present and clinically installed like unsuitable calcinated washers in all ranks within the NHS.

My work and ethics are my choice, but a choice I have made long-time ago. To the NHS staff that I worked with i.e. the admin staff that would book appointments, clear my clinical schedule as needed, etc., I am grateful and I remember them fondly. To the NHS's staff patients, I feel like they are a representative cohort of patients in their own right, and I do wish them well. Such facts still cannot be classified as I feeling gratitude towards the NHS Trust and/or the NHS overall, also, pretty certain that my lack of gratitude towards that NHS Trust or the NHS as an organisation, will absolutely never change. It is now a very well established fact.

Below my email that the British Association of Counselling and Psychotherapy (BACP) deemed as my harassment, whereas at point of sending that email, the NHS Trust and Occupational Health (OH) chief, Iain Dockerty had contacted me in writing and on call on several occasions with suggestions of breach of data of my clients (remember that my clients were the NHS staff and my honorary employment contract was finished with liability on that contract clearly stipulated in the contract dated 11th March 2015 - the breach of data was in fact Croydon Health Services NHS Trust). Contact from Iain was via three letters from DPO office at the Trust, legal department at the Trust (that in fact were employed to respond to I and my liability that the NHS Trust was suggesting and implying though its correspondence to I) and OH head who was eager for me to book an appointment with Emma Ulysses to discuss the NHS Trust own breach and fraudulent data failure in regards to their service files and knowingly that I had no insight at all on what the OH service had breached. Plus my contract was finalised six months prior or so. I was never involved in the NHS Trust service data and everything that I provided was done by my own templates and my own self-made reported data. Under no principles I could have helped the service other than private consultancy and so I issued an invoice to Iain Dockerty that he declined and verbally abused me upon receipt. The expectation was clear, I shall make myself available to both Iain Dockerty and Emma Ulysses' demands for free, like slavery and servitude or I shall suffer their repercussions/reprimands. I say the NHS Trust " their records", because I never accessed any of the OH 's service files. Never during six years' time as a honorary consultant. My notes to the service are and were made confidential and coded on my own templates. My records on sessions barely two sentences per one analytical hour. Not because I could not write essays on each and every analytic encounter, mostly due to my photographic memory, I can recall an entire session verbatim even today from a session that took place in 2015, but because I am taking very seriously patient and analyst confidentiality. Except when I decide that a former client is attacking me, which is the case with both Iain and Emma and the NHS Trust. I have analysed Emma and I have analysed Iain and next volume is about them on two chapters. What to keep in mind as my principle of analytic practice, I have always considered that the NHS staff were my patients and I did not think it essential to report other than my own methods in session records that I was putting forward to the service. Never had I breached client's confidentiality in my reports in any service and never will. I can group together pattern of study and recall to minutiae of session, but there is no way in such circumstances that former patients would recognise themselves. It would be a lie for anyone to suggest that. Not a coincidence, a lie. Returning to the incident with Iain Dockerty in 2021, over a period of two months I was receiving, via post, letters from the NHS Trust's various departments at my home address – confidential data under GDPR 2018 rules and an evident breach of all legislation including employment legislation – needless to say that such departments were liable for making contact with me outside the honorary contract and in doing so, the whole NHS was liable. And so, I filed another three invoices with the NHS Trust, my action catapulted specific individuals, Emma Ulysses, Iain Dockerty and Ashley Irving paralegal to commence a series of attacks and defamation on my ethical stance with effectively, the NHS Trust self-incriminating on all aspects mentioned by their allegations against I to the BACP. It seems that instead of the NHS Trust to look closely in the mirror that I put up for them for six years, decided to break through it like the elephant in the room that they were. Sad, but not unusual: therapy does many things, including what is called: acting out on defenses and with failing therapy meaning, also, falling on your own sword as rupture – which is the case with the three individuals, the BACP, the Trust and the NHS at large in regards to I, the actual analyst.

1st Email

to:CH-TR.dpo@nhs.net, "Ulysses Emma (CROYDON HEALTH SERVICES NHS TRUST)" <emma.ulysses@nhs.net>, "Docherty Iain (CROYDON HEALTH SERVICES NHS TRUST)" <iain.docherty@nhs.net>,ashley.irving@nhs.net, ch-tr.legalservices@nhs.net

date: Jul 31, 2021, 5:13 PM

subject: Fwd: Invoice payable with immediate effect mailed-by:gmail.com

Hi There,

Thank you for your continuous request for services. As you are aware my services for large corporations including the NHS Trust Croydon Health Services is not free of charge, therefore I have attached an invoice for services requested up to date on three occasions. Croydon Health Services used to be an honorary client, however, not honorary since 2020. I understand that you are still unclear of your records and you have made contact with us without cause other than request services at our current business rates. Please forward this invoice and your request letters to us to your accounts for immediate payment.

Many thanks.

Madalina Day

One attachment • Scanned by Gmail

2nd email

to:CH-TR.dpo@nhs.net,

"Ulysses Emma (CROYDON HEALTH SERVICES NHS TRUST)"
<emma.ulysses@nhs.net>,
"Docherty Iain (CROYDON HEALTH SERVICES NHS TRUST)"
<iain.docherty@nhs.net>,
ashley.irving@nhs.net,
CH-TR.legalservices@nhs.net

date:Jul 31, 2021, 5:13 PM

subject:Fwd: Invoice payable with immediate effect

mailed-by:gmail.com

The Analyst: *There is a bounty on my head*

Sat, Jul 31, 2021, 5:13 PM

to mday, Ulysses, Docherty, ashley.irving, CH-TR.legalservices, CH-TR.dpo, New

Attached invoice and it is now 17 months outstanding. On the same legal issue and imminent criminal charges filed against the below, I will now make a formal request SAR for letters submitted by DPO to Madalina Day in relation to a honorary contract and all investigations against Madalina Day with dates/names involved and reasons for contact outside the honorary contract. The SAR request is with immediate effect and DPO at Croydon Health services has 21 days to respond. The invoice is now on 20% adding interest on a monthly basis exclusive of VAT.I have attached invoices prompted by actions of Emma Ulysses, Iain Docherty and Ashley Irving to Data protection at Croydon Health Services with being contacted on three occasions. The attached invoices are overdue and need payment with immediate effect. The invoices are not including any compensation and damages claimed under criminal offences committed by specific individuals nominally: Iain Docherty head of OH between 2017 and including 2021, Emma Ulysses Counsellor Lead offences committed between 2017 and including 2021, Data Protection Officer at Croydon Health Services NHS Trust during 2020 and Legal Team at Croydon Health Services NHS Trust Ashley Irving and the Trust itself.
Invoices attached.
Failure to make such payments within the next 5 working days and by 4th of August 2021, all individuals and the organisation is going to be referred to various Debt collection agencies and the invoices are going to be filed as evidence against criminal acts committed by said individuals and their employment organisation under the below offences: The offences under modern slavery are:

- Slavery, servitude, and forced or compulsory labour
- Human trafficking
- Meaning of exploitation
- Committing offence with intent to commit offence under section 2

Slavery, Servitude and forced or compulsory labour: A person commits this offence if:

- The person holds another in slavery or servitude, and circumstances are that the person knows or ought to know that the other is held in slavery or servitude
- The person requires another to perform forced or compulsory labour, and circumstances are such that the person knows or ought to know the other is being required to perform forced or compulsory labour

One attachment • Scanned by Gmail Reply all Forward

Chapter 2: An outreach community therapy service in East London

2.1.Case 1. Abel

My first trainee: *reading unconscious and going back to the source, the story of Abel on West End Lane and I*

Disclosure statement: ***The below account is an example of study: Abel exists, all identifiers preserve patient's anonymous status, and confidentiality of "third" in the room.***

Almost nine years ago I was invited to a private premiere of David Cronenberg's film about Spielrein, Jung and Freud "A Dangerous Method" hosted by the Confederation for Analytical Psychology, followed by a conference discussion with renowned writers such as Lisa Appignanesi.(https://www.andrewsamuels.com/a-dangerous-method-private-showing-and-conference-discussion/).   Appignanesi was known to me from five years prior and by reading her books and attending live conference discussions i.e. Freud's Women. The private screening and conference were offered as the fourth Andrew Samuels lecture. (http://www.ruthwilliams.org.uk/conference_flyer.pdf). That event remained an important reference to a discussion on meanings of therapeutic relationship as a "third" in a room. Analyses proposed during that conference came back to me almost unequivocally when I was asked to participate in all trainings since, but it also helped in rethinking all past contributions to readings of Klein (Melanie) and how futile a possible dynamic comes into a block when two analysts (think) they speak same (analytic) language, and how that then can be modelled into a different modality of conversing. Abel, my first trainee psychoanalytic study is by far (or rather) one good example of such an overcoming block. A decade earlier, I envisaged such a possibility, cumulated with writings on how a split between Freud and Jung happened, to I, portraying clear (mis) understandings on how a "spiritual" X are unaccounted: here* and now* become the only norm of time orientation*. It has long being clear to me that unconscious road can be recreated beyond a memory lane - it is sufficient one to account for A.I. possibilities, and if that is deemed insufficient, than **counting strategy** comes into the fore to predict a fact known* from a fact* predictable. Chess is one example - predictability is key, but chess moves are successful only when an unpredictable plays various unimaginable moves ahead and simultaneously accounts for several developed contingency plans at once. Photographic memory is **KEY**, not for recall alone, but for trials of building future blocks. That is one identified difference between chess and psychoanalysis, in my clinical opinion: chess plays ahead, always, it also gives moves' ideas to opponents to lay beliefs that things have, are and will develop a certain way. Psychoanalysis reads in the past, negotiates sometimes successfully. I would like to think that my therapy does both. Abel and I, was a good cause, we created a play without a dynamic possible and I am certain that Abel will never play chess, but it proved to be my best learning ever allowing for an understanding in the rift caused between Freud and Jung. More importantly why Klein had such a hard time when moving to London earlier in her career.

References:

Klein, M.(1967) notes and letters

The Analyst: *There is a bounty on my head*

2.2.Case 2. Bernadette

Relationships: What are they/them?

Disclosure statement: *The below account is an example of study: Bernadette exists, all identifiers preserve patient's anonymous status, and confidentiality of "third" in the room.*

One evening in October 2013, I was in my bedroom with dim light on, completing a last minute case study on Acceptance and Commitment Therapy (ACT) module, and I could see on my side left corner of my laptop screen an invite to part take into a quiz for finding best assessment screening measures resources. As it happened, I completed that quiz in less than timeframe provided and I felt grateful on that quiz opportunity and participation. My evening was insufficiently focussed on reflecting on my work. When all were put to rest with that quiz, I had a regroup on my mind with the help of one advert and I ventured out from psychology forums and forms, to some other quizzes ready available coming up on my screen. One such prospective enquiry came from MIX95 security services and that very same screen can be accessed here: https://www.mix95.govestr.uk59/careers/quizzes. I took the investigative challenge first and I have barely passed 2 out of 28 score - within fractions of seconds, I re/attempted same challenge within seconds and got 3 out of 28. It must be said that there was no intention on furthering my analytical skills at that time. I do not gamble, I do not have a gambling mind, and I only complete Sudoku on my commute to work to pass the time, but at very core of me there is no desire to unnecessarily challenge my mind. I now think that part of me changed after that reflective evening. A feeling was born from an understanding whether there is an aspect of my logic that is able to compartmentalize and re/evaluate types of involvement in different relationships on a dynamic between personal and professional levels. There is a question as to how best define that capacity, an ability, and to be quite so clear and distinct about differences between personal and professional life.

Readers might wonder how, why and what Bernadette's story has anything to do with relationships and what are they/them question from chapter title. My answer is that all such events from that evening are relatively significant and Bernadette's expose, presents a self-introspection and, equally, a concluding remark: "difference of professional and personal level are collapsed in an investigative enquiry and when having to disentangle or rather pursue what matters most, it may be a difficult task."

Relationships are hard, a constant negotiation between **wants**, **haves** and *dreams of one with dreams of two*, etc.; relationships are also hard because an individual understanding and self-growth must always check in with values and where she/he is positioning herself/himself within a larger structure of society. Yesterday evening I went through some old e-files, and one email had as subject line: *attachment*! When opened and read, I realised that it was in fact an outline of a book reference from 2012, titled "*The science of persuasion*" by Robert Cialdini. A great text, extremely informative on arbitration of not the private and public self, but personal and more personal. What, if anything, can be seen as an incentive to persuasion? Perhaps we all have a life time to find out exactly that.

References:

Cialdini, R. (2007). *Influence: the psychology of persuasion*. Harper Collins: New York.

Chapter 3: An outreach community therapy service in West London

3.1.Case 1. Chance

A case of clinical supervision: How do you chose your therapist and why it is important? Relating choice of supervision with choice of therapist.

Disclosure statement: *The below account is an example of study: Chance exists, all identifiers preserve patient's anonymous status, and confidentiality of "third" in the room.*

It is always a puzzle as to how can one start advertising for oneself in a profession that one represents more than a mere person, but comes with the "baggage" of being an institution in itself. I always had peer clinical supervision in place from that was custom made with combining a two roles - managerial and clinical; to start with, it was perceived more as clinical discussions even if with an acknowledgement that there were several clinical aspects and clinical reasoning involved transcending from a theoretical stance practice to patient based cluster of difficulties. In all previous clinical settings paid or unpaid peer supervision was always on offer with arrangements for private practice as a separate set of supervision and so on. If not careful, one can get quite so lost in so many clinical supervisors' views, approaches and ways of working. And I thought to my/self – for many a years now – well, there is not only a necessity, ethical requirement, but a form of support. All in equal measure to both need and demand.

Today I have met with a new colleague for clinical consultancy and it was by choice, I have searched on line availability after contacting several others fellow colleagues from previous projects and psychotherapeutic settings. It must be said that it felt as a new pathway opening up with hope and excitement, and not in the least being much needed. Unlike with so many other previous experiences in having to decide on supervision and question as to whether or not my choice is best approach, today I were face with a different type of choice. My training at its foundational stage is analysis and it has always been clear to me that my practice is never going to be about a specific modality, but about combining all knowledge and experience accumulated over decades. And yet today, during peer consultancy, such experience and knowledge gradually became reduced to decisions as to whether a clinician trained in strictly psychodynamic model is in any way going to be able to respond to my way of working and my current patients' needs. Would my third eye (supervisor) trained only in one modality would truly be able to enable and bring something new to my work and my client's work? Question unanswered. Thinking back at session, there are countless moments when the supervisor was preoccupied with offering examples on various gender and race identity of her other colleagues that she is working with, that and also self-defining herself through various criteria: white, middleclass etc. How am I going to relate my current work with that appreciation? What is the most essential point of reference in our profession, and how are we to take out or incorporate differences by naming such differences concisely, directly and deliberately from the start? I find myself in my so called consultancy session becoming empathic to my colleague, and more as a listener than analysing, there was a sense of saying – this is terribly wrong and is really going nowhere. I keep wondering, surely is going to get somehow better and yet, I already know that there is no way it can. Am I going to once again be polite and accept that there are always going to be available ways to work with differences even if next time I could just perhaps re/direct session on means as to what my client work actually requires it? Would I just give it one more try before saying no, thank you. My relational way of working is saying yes, of course, anything is possible. My stronger sense of self and knowing what it is needed right now, at this moment in time, are saying no. Perhaps staying with such differences it is a start in itself. It was pleasing to know that we trained at similar settings and perhaps there is much to offer in that sense. After session, I followed up with an appointment for skin care - just an informal complimentary skin treatment - more preparatory for potential harshness of autumn and lack of sunlight. I left that room making an appointment for two weeks' time, equally wondering whether or not is truly going to help. However, for facial treatment I left a deposit and I am bound to return. With consultancy session, as with many other experiences as a professional, I am certain to attend even if for addressing some of the challenges in my mind about my current work. I also know that there is no such thing as a bad analytic session and how I feel now is more about peer supervision given that I am not long from wanting to start on that quest, I thought it may wait until January, but it looks like I had a successful start on that today, instead. After all I am all about learning and never giving up. Now, I need to find a course to enrol on that type of training and advertise it as such. So that is what is next for me, that and the skincare treatment in two weeks' time.

The Analyst: *There is a bounty on my head*

3.2. Case 2. Alip

Is decency a trait: yes, decency is…; making the case for practice reflections in analytical writing

Disclosure statement: *The below account is an example of study: Alip exists, all identifiers preserve patient's anonymous status, and confidentiality of "third" in the room.*

This story is ahead of its time and yet, perhaps not timely enough for what it's about to say. Also it is **highly possible that it may be first and last story of this format and subject matter**: an evaluation on considering whether or not decency or decency on a measurement scale fits best with my scope and purpose of writing and making all such writing freely available.

Is it for ourselves or for our readers? **Both? Perhaps not, but I would think it more along the lines as to "how can I help" question**. If when specifically answering that question, we entertained a guideline that most of our writings are based on spontaneous ideas that we may think as both relevant and interesting to a larger audience - **such consideration made a sufficient case or it has sufficient merit for continuing with our writing on these pages** - however, recently it feels less urgent that a large audience of readership can benefit from our writing hence decency, becomes an ethical question in this case, here, I mean. Or **rather pondering on scope at large, such an hesitation can only be applied to specific part - content** that may be classed as less relevant at particular points in time.

All our ideas are beautifully developed - and not all inclusive of specific client material or cases and certainly not all about specific encounters. Things are much, much simpler: I have an idea! Naturally I am told, it happens, most probably because, ultimately, various forms of acquired knowledge had been collated, evaluated, combined and assessed - **several sources of information had reached an overload status over a significant period of time** - interdisciplinary science and practice based knowledge that had been processed and tested against my experience and knowledge assessed against guidelines of good practice within my profession - if it is about a professional matter. And then yes, I have an idea! One morning, recently, when readapting best guidance policy for our practice - decency, as a point of reference came to mind. It felt quite obvious that any principle for **good practice and when writing a guideline, would have letter of stone on decency -** when I reformulated that idea, I've wondered if decency is a facet of one's character; than that followed on with a consideration on my knowledge and practice of individual differences including personality traits and eventually all questioning was rephrased as: **"Is decency a trait"?** Just so I can test further my thinking, I recalled various writings (science) on predictability of behaviour/conduct. When Googled such terms, most interestingly, my idea returned scholarly articles on decency and leadership (Hudson, 2020) **the two concepts grouped together alongside IQ and EQ with Decency being suggested as a third measurable dimension when assessing leadership skills.** But that is not all that I had in mind. I simply questioned if Decency is a stable, measurable characteristic, similar to concept of trait (personality) and **not an attitude - much much debate on similarities and dissimilarities between traits and attitudes!**

And then, I realised that, in practice terms, decency could be termed and determined against adherence to ethical conduct and good practice principles (to a larger extent exhibited behaviour, hence conduct and cognizant application of such ethical principles). **At a personal level, decency is not so well nuanced - encounters with what could be termed as decency also have met with a (un) known deceit -** all life experienced - and that created some really difficult feelings. At this point, creating a guideline, that holds a question on nature of decency, seems less and less plausible. As such, it is decided that decency, conceptually, is a matter of self-interpretation of a situation or event.

For instance, my **December 2020 offered readership possibility** of feedback on aspect to its writing and I had an overwhelming response as to how **I should continue in offering the best that there is as a form of support**; two ways feedback on my practice with clients/patients is overwhelmingly positive and yet, I know that there is so much more that I want to do and accomplish.

Decency suggests humbleness and mentalising - I am absolutely certain that **I am both humble and I practice mentalising** - whether or not this had been a successfully synchronised project, remains to be seen.

The Analyst: *There is a bounty on my head*

Decency and leadership makes much sense because I can certainly relate to that **entirely and positively in all that I hold as knowledge and experience** - such examples are countless. Are there any situations when there is a need to be in a deeper reflection about it? Certainly, yes, if and when decency also means acknowledgement of being wrong sometimes, perhaps overly protective or reassessing a form of behaviour that has new knowledge to a previous interpretation. But, I think that one of the most important aspects of both decency and leadership, is a capability of predicting future events and then preventatively acting on such knowledge - from my **professional** experience one example stands out most and it happened such **a long time ago that it cannot be named.**

I conclude that decency is in fact a characteristic of one's conduct that need to be measured against multiple environments, events and interactions - crossings between personal and professional - however, decency cannot be construed as an evidence-base construct at one specific point in time, nor as an ultimate measurable, stable trait or characteristic of one's form of conduct on a single vantage point.

Writing this …and then questioning: is this writing decent enough to be published?

Answer: ",,, **it feels like it falls short of in so many ways, and with that acknowledgement in mind, publishing this, it's perhaps the most decent thing to do,** at least on my part .

Chapter 4: An outreach community therapy service in Central London

4.1.Case 1. John

15th June 2021 Preventative work and its importance – The case of John

Disclosure statement: ***The below account is an example of study: John exists, all identifiers preserve patient's anonymous status, and confidentiality of "third" in the room.***

I had no intention on writing more for John case 21 but, then again, circumstances halfway through the month called for a change; I had a few distinct encounters with risk assessments and preventative work during the past few weeks and one such case was John. Risk assessments are continuous processes incorporated in any work with clients/patients. Such a process starts at assessment or initial sessions, or upon referrals from other services, and continue throughout the work. Risk assessment is a highly significant process - safeguarding the patients, whilst monitoring any fluctuations/changes in psychotherapeutic focus. Recent work prompted me to revisit suicide prevention work as a conceptual map and rethink all my therapeutic encounters with suicide prevention, allowing for an identification of possible themes/patterns in all such narratives. The result was writing an article for Counselling Directory that had to be simplified and much of importance had to be reformulated. The article in its entirety can be found here: https://www.counselling-directory.org.uk/memberarticles/suicide-prevention-and-anger-in-they-said-and-i-said

The article is accessible to anyone with an interest in mental health practice, independently of being a potential client, service collaboration or not. It is a free space.

Main theme identified when rethinking preventative work across 8 services in both private and public practice was in fact a phrase:

"They said and I said" ...

The Analyst: *There is a bounty on my head*

Eight services, countless patients without a distinct criteria of forming a client group except for a deeply felt uncontained anger, and years of battling with mental health challenges.

Ironically, by putting forward "They said and I said" phrase, it can be argued that it is about my practice and specific psychotherapeutic encounters - *they* . I am aware of that, however, client group is not a valid argument - because in the room there is not an *I* from a therapist/psychotherapist point of view/you - not in psychodynamic terms (Winnicott may want to come forth and discuss countertransference, and a therapist awareness of intense feelings), in CBT terms there is only a collaboration, empirical collaboration between the therapist and the client, and all other potential models would not so much acknowledge the therapeutic relationship as essence to the therapy. So the mentioned article is, as much as it can be, a professional opinion evidence-base from across several services with one element in common: all such clients/patients were long term patients for over 12 months in therapy. The cases I am referring to, are extreme and I have worked with such patients for years. All patients of different services - majority of such services offer outreach work in the community, specialist services such as personality disorders, neurodevelopmental atypical cases with extreme life trauma and many more. The article was based on all such encounters and it includes cases of onset/ clinical depression - severe psychological challenges. It is a warning really: when the talk about **they and I** - exists, it can mean recall of **severe trauma** - from a psychotherapeutic point of view. It may be that there are coping mechanisms in place, such as self-developed resilience, or built -in safe defenses. But, in cases of clinical depression and if prescribed medication, any triggers in life situations would leave you further exposed with a real need for an appreciation of talking therapy being immense. The phrase, at face value may mean nothing, but in psychological terms, it is or it can be devastating.

It goes beyond a felt or perceived discrimination, with feelings of anger that can exceed humanly tolerance levels. It can also be about questioning identity and membership to group/ belonging; it can be about an unprocessed closure event and despondence about similar experiences felt as same. It can be about preventative psychology too - even if it is read in so few words.

The Analyst: *There is a bounty on my head*

The below excerpt is what has been reformulated from the original article on Counselling Directory and I think it important:

"They said and I said and Anger.

Anger is never a feeling that can ultimately be left unaccounted for; anger is survival only when not left adrift to ravage one's mind, because when it does, it turns onwards and against life itself. Anger is only a powerful emotion associated to living when processed and fully understood. Do not push it aside and do not ignore it, it becomes they – to start with - and then it becomes the I, with a great potential of annihilating your desire to live. The most extreme cases and the most encountered cases of such transitions are when They are distinctly different from the I - it could be through culture or any or several criteria of difference. Obstacles of culture and language are, unfortunately, some of the quickest ways of identifying and designating they - not necessarily wishfully, but it can happen when one experience discrimination perhaps not overtly felt or immediately felt. The other or combination of any other 9 protected criteria could form a distinct and clear sequence of events of **they and I** as notable experiences in whatever setting and format. Please think about that before you decide that mental health conditions are always primary to life experiences. Often, are not. Gender, sex, sexuality, race, can be primary felt challenging experiences in a repetitive and hurtful sense of **They and I**.

Developmental stages and ways of communication can play significant roles in all such events. Interpersonal potentials involved in communication, i.e., personality traits or neurodevelopmental factors are highly relevant to a **they and I** communication- please do take your time to fully understand yourself from whatever angle, school of thought or chosen way to do so. The world is never about **they** - I have learned that much. It took years of therapy to some of the patients that have worked with me, to unpack the **they** and reveal to themselves what they meant by **they**. Sometimes **they** representing one or two or three separate individuals or organizations at large. Sometimes all such individuals to be recognised as good and bad not only good and not only bad.

They can only exist when the "I "decides to let them exist and take over. The I and You are what really matters. YOU Matter. The dialogue between *They and I* can only be useful to discover **you,** at least in psychological, psychotherapeutic terms. And your healthy sentence could sound like: "When I used to think that there was a They and I, I later realised that there was an I and someone else saying that I was a YOU to them."

Winnicott(1949) states:

"…The identifications and tendencies belonging to an analyst's personal experiences and personal development which provide the positive setting for his analytic work and make his work different in quality from that of any other analyst…. I distinguish the truly objective counter-transference, or if this is difficult, the analyst's love and hate in reaction to the actual personality and behaviour of the patient, based on objective observation. I suggest that if an analyst is to analyse psychotics or anti-socials he must be able to be so thoroughly aware of the counter-transference that he can sort out and study his <u>objective reactions</u> to the patient. These will include hate. Counter-transference phenomena will at times be the important things in the analysis. "(p.69)

References:

Winnicott, D.W. (1949). "Hate in the Counter-Transference". *International Journal of. Psychoanalysis.*, Vol. 30. Pp 69-74.

The Analyst: *There is a bounty on my head*

4.2. Case 2. Kate

The case of a failed Matrix and childhood memories; stories why are important...

Disclosure statement: ***The below account is an example of study: Kate exists, all identifiers preserve patient's anonymous status, and confidentiality of "third" in the room.***

"Not so long ago I have been involved with two cases in HM Central Family Court – a case of Public Law and a case of Private law. Both cases involved a child, two parents and a Local Authority from a London borough. As the cases were progressing from one stage to the next, several family Court Judges were involved, different solicitors and different Counsel for each hearing. The Applicant changed from being a parent to being local Authority respectively, the parents and the child become respondents from applicants in same legal proceedings. The case changed from Private Law to Public Law.

Most legal teams formed from one representative to two representatives and each had assigned their Counsel in Court at different stages in the process. The child had been assigned by the Court a Guardian so what it started as a family matter between two parents, it now became a Circus of the state. What I failed to mentioned is that, the child in question was a child discriminated against by the Local Authority and during Family Court Proceedings there was a Court order by Special Educational Needs and Disability Tribunal ordering the local Authority to initiate an Educational Health Care Plan for the child in question.

All throughout this process there was a parent fighting for the rights of the child through recognition and application of Equality Act 2010. The Family Court instead, invited the party - that were at failure of responding to the needs of the child - to become the very Authority to take action and report on the child's welfare and safeguarding. The abuser and the discriminator was legally ordered by a Judge in Central Family Court to part-take to the proceedings as the protector and applicant to a child care arrangements proceedings. That party was the Local Authority and aligned, like an appendices, was the father to the proceedings. The Local Authority and the father made good teams with an army of lawyers, solicitors and counsels.

The Analyst: *There is a bounty on my head*

The mother, self-represented in court had much to hope for. her very existence and when being told in court that she had no chance, at no point in the process, but in spite, she continued her fight – a lost battle, seen by many and expressed in Court by the very Judges:

"dear Ms…..X., I am not so sure you understand the gravity of this situation!" –

The mother, by which now she was in full comprehension to the seriousness of the situation responded:

…I am aware, as I am aware of you and who/m you represent" – You see, the mother, had a faith in the judgment of a Judge, not because she was a female Judge, but because the mother believed in objectivity". The mother thought: " if this Judge cannot be trusted upon, no one can!"

The case did not have a finality as such, the female Judge failed, abruptly and without a cause, she was emotional during final judgement and made it personal - The Judge proved that she could not uphold herself in the very seat that she was occupying and was ruthless and without a cause ordered a child to come to Court and be told that his wishes are worth nothing, that his feelings are worth nothing, that his life is worth nothing and that she, the Judge, has the power to make him feel worthless, confused and scared. The child, felt exactly that for fractions of seconds and many hours, the only survival way was readings and relating to his mother's words:

"Life is a breathing exercise – minute by minute – and that is the only way forward.. The child texted to the mother:

"*I love you mum*

And don't worry

About me

I love you

The Analyst: *There is a bounty on my head*

And things are going to be ok

Not your fault

Not mine

Its no ones

......

I'm going to sleep now

And iv been thinking about the minute by minute thing

A lot

And 1 min im in court one minute im playing 1 minute my dads trying to perswade me that he didn't start all this

I love you mum

To the moon and back then back again

I'll see you soon

1 minute I'm here then I'll be with you

Hugging you

I love you night"

The above are the words of the child, crushed to the power of a failed State, a failed System but more importantly a failed Nation and a failed understanding of meanings of Culture. I have tried to explain this to the child that there is no System to blame, as the so called "system" is made up of people and legislation, hence cannot be a failure of the system. People and legislation are accountable for as we all are responsible in our daily lives, for everything we do and not do. The moment we awake, is the moment we become responsible, the moment we stand (on two feet) or not is the moment we gain recognition for who we are - we become accountable to Law and the Law becomes accountable to us. The State is not a one way street. Our freedom is not one way street, our rights are not one way street. Our humanity is not one way street. Our compassion is not one way street. Our acceptance is not our one way street. Our political voice is not one way street. Therefore our children and their voices are not one way street, and their power and ways of being from one generation to the next, is beyond one way street – **it is our legacy**.

The child in the story was failed, failed by a parent, failed by a solicitor, failed by its Counsel, failed by it Secondary school, failed by its Court of Justice, failed by a Family Court Judge, failed by Social Services, failed by all around including his mother, a parent that had and has nothing to go by other than a belief: a belief that in a world like ours, you need to be resilient and grow of nothing because nothing is there to offer, a belief that we all seek understanding and find resolution with what we have and what we explore, the belief that answers are within us – even if sometimes the reach is painful and or uncomfortable – we become and we are what we believe.

The story continues beyond the Family Court and First-tier Tribunal Court, it is out/there with a child being ordered to come to Court and against his wishes to change residency and have no further contact with one parent. The moral of this story is not about injustice and inhumanity, but about reflective practice. This article is for you, potential clients/patients reaching out for support and guidance. The moral of above story is about resilience and self-reliance.

The story is about belief, belief in a power above a state of being and belief in who you are. Therapy is one process for exploring that, becoming self-aware of who you are and where you want to be, offering a possibility to question, question your resilience and answer to your very explorations:

"Am I taking this journey in life or am I suggesting someone else is making this journey for me and or instead of me?"

The Analyst: *There is a bounty on my head*

This subchapter is entitled stories and not injustice or "failing through the cracks of a failed system and a failed state" because, when I have made the decision to become a practitioner of psychotherapy and analysis, I have made a vow to myself:

"I shall never, absolutely never cease to reflect on my "humanity" and that, to me, is my one way street. **It is as simple as that.**

I do not suggest that reflective practice is the ultimate way to heaven or becoming a better person, but I do strongly and sincerely suggest that it's a starting point into becoming and being an adult no matter what life confronts you with."

Chapter 5: An University counselling and mentoring service in North London

5.1. Case 1. Alison

A case of Truth: November 2019 – Why stories are important: reality and narratives – the truth within and the truth without

Disclosure statement: ***The below account is an example of study: Alison exists, all identifiers preserve patient's anonymous status, and confidentiality of "third" in the room.***

The following events are described as had been proposed to me on real terms during an episode of disclosure and then agreed consent for publishing; it involves a child, parents and a local authority service – it is about a negotiation of parental responsibility and there are audio files and written accounts by all involved with the child in question that verifies and sustains this reporting – there are no questions over interpretation as it re/accounts an experiential living of an event where democratic discernment and human rights come to a holt and/ or block. Therefore, such events are than reinterpreted and bestowed upon decision making responsible public and civilian bodies/and all concerned. The overall results are patiently assessed and outcomes relieved of doubt in their interpretation. Unfortunate
life events to all such individuals are seen as a boomerang to their decision making process; life experiences of one child for a collapse of corruption, lack of integrity and professionalism - a psychoanalytic thread of black matter being traced throughout.
09/08/2018 – deliberate misinformation/ dishonesty regarding home visit in making contact with a child as part of statutory duty and ISO – the information provided by social services/worker had no evidence being relayed in a Court of Justice as part of Social Work Evidence to Family Court. A statement of Truth has been signed with full acknowledgement of no such evidence to all stated being provided. On the contrary there are audio files and evidence from various sources that not only contradict such evidence but incriminate various other individuals and institutions at large including non-resident parent that committed theft in removing personal identification documents of a child from the resident parent's property in the

presence of a local police, local authority services, privately employed educational tutors and witness of resident parent. Such criminal law pertinent crime was directed and conducted by all attended during a so called safeguarding check conducted by local authority officers to a referral made on 7th of February 2018 from two points of reference: 1. secondary school UCL Academy whereas staff indicated that child in question should be provided with a yellow bag for managing his nosebleeds and excluding the child from all activities including his football team due to absences regarding his medical condition and 2. Local General Practitioner Swiss Cottage Medical Centre partner Sarah Smith making a referral because the resident parent in question decided to pursue a privately paid assessment of the child to various reference points including an Educational Child Psychologist, Anna Freud Emotional Psychotherapy Service and Psychological Service that the child had been NHS serviced at for his nosebleeds.

The reasoning for Dr. Sarah Smith as a GP were that the parent in question would not be sufficiently educated in what it is the best interest for her child (13teen years of age at the time – the power of the state should intervene when a parent decides to investigate and explore their child's difficulties that would go beyond what is seemed or deemed merited by a GP that had never met the child, had no real comprehension on the child's lived medical experience and no real grasp on his medical background including an inflicted gross and critical malpractice by the NHS staff at child's birth under the form of injecting a four days old infant with an antiviral HIV medication ten times the dosage allowed to an infected adult population. The child in question had no viral infection and or exposure to that virus and by administering such a drug without a cause and to a dosage never administered to an adult infected population, the NHS were introspectively on stand by for their own malpractice. The inexplicable nosebleeds and difficulties of family life that the child in question experienced from his four days of birth since the accident, were than reformulated in a different narrative by the GP practice (NHS owned), social services in the service of both the NHS and local Authority Government and the non-resident parent that was - at the time of this happening – filing in Family court for reduced maintenance child and spousal maintenance payments. After the inflicted malpractice by the NHS, the four days old infant survived and was returned to his parents, however, the parental relationship and the marriage did not survived. The mother never agreed to the *laisse fair* attitude of the father towards the infant exhibited by the father during a meeting with the Royal Free Hospital staff when consequences and impact and a way forward for the child were requested as a consequence of the hospital malpractice towards the new born.

During such a meeting, the mother (rightly so) requested that assurances of the child not being affected are taking place with requesting from the drug company further information on the drug and from the hospital assurances that such an event had no medical effect on the child. What the mother did no request at that time were that other consequences were written off such as a frequent blood tests and investigations take place on a regular basis. The impact and consequences of the malpractice had been flourished negatively within the marital relationship and the newly born, the parental relationship did not survive beyond three years mark – mostly due to constant divergences between the couple in regards of the best interest of the child. The second point of reference were intense and frequent nosebleeds from the infant that were not manifesting as a consequence of external factors but internal factors. The NHS never repeated the blood tests and when upon request from the mother at three years of age and five years of age, were declared as normal, only to be told six years later that the blood tests conducted at five years of age were never performed with the blood samples being lost.

The moral of the above story is for reader to discern, what is relevant for the purpose of this re/account is "telling the story" and meanings attached to a lived experience that from biographical to a narrative becomes a reality of many. This is not about accountability or shifting sands so to say, there are many perspectives and timelines with a history of their own, more importantly it is about a legacy, a legacy that in the eyes of many is yet to be resolved.

Why stories are important in therapy is exactly about that, creating possibilities of re/examination of deeply rooted understandings, embedded and entrenched ways of being that could find emotional and comprehensible tangible ways for clarification.

Stories in therapy are forms of relocating and prompting oneself to an imaginary scenario, eliciting ways of emotionally thinking, compatible to one's ways of being. Stories in therapy - as a technique - allows for innovation, creativity, retrospection of self-acceptance, compassion and offering forms of mentalizing with the outside world, others and a sense of self.

Recently, I have created an exercise about grounding and a re/assessment of values and meaning of self. It is simple and invites the patient/client to describe herself/himself as he or she or they would exist as a country – an agency – an organisation rather than a mere individual. What would such a description bring to light? What would such a sense of self, recreated under such terms, would reveal? A story of self-mapped out within a wider context; how emotionally involved one may feel during such an exercise? What corners of one's mind may look like depicted in such form? Would one decide that one is an island and or a small country with well-defined borders and a clear internal organisation and external ways of co-existing? Such an exercise would allow for self-introspection and exploration - it can be used at any stage in one's life when shadows of uncertainty colours one life or simply when one needs to be reminded of a sense of self.

The Analyst: *There is a bounty on my head*

5.2. Case 2. Yishmael

A case of Belonging: Yishmael and Europe

Disclosure statement: *The below account is an example of study: Yishmael exists, all identifiers preserve patient's anonymous status, and confidentiality of "third" in the room.*

On the 5th of April 1968, *New Statesman* published a book review entitled *The Search* by V.S. Pritchett.

I received a copy of that review from original print 42 years later, unrequested, but nevertheless, enormously appreciated. The original printed newspaper cuttings were included with a second-hand purchase of an autobiography entitled "Belonging" by Willa Muir. I have ordered that book from an independent book seller in 2010. I often wondered why the person that had been so kindred, kind and generous made such a gesture. I could not know for sure that it was deliberate, and it was by choice to think that it must have been.

The book itself has great value as it stands - I was accustomed to readings by W.M and her previous writings - acutely aware of several other literary implications of both the work itself and the author's personal life; Willa was married to Edwin Muir, a prolific Scottish poet and together with Willa both were renowned for translations of Kafka. I first read W.M in early 2000 and I felt quite invested in her account in *Imagined Corners*, published in 1935. Often, I related to her characters, biographical nevertheless, and when receiving an original printed newspaper review on her memoir sometime in 2010, to me, it felt quite significant.

Books, for I, are most valuable, most probably because as a child, I was told that books are also a form of resistance to oppression. I witnessed that in so many forms and at so many times, whole libraries and archives being burned down just because one regime, and one dictatorship could not allow written word to manifest, exist and become an educated legacy.

People were not allowed to know, to educate themselves, to want, to aspire, to wish, to think for themselves and to have freedom of speech: simply to exist as sole governors of their own mind and life.

The Analyst: *There is a bounty on my head*

Belonging to such a life, being raised and educated in such conditions and considerations of what it is supposed to be a nurturing environment, can make one a philosopher for life. The matrix of oppression or felt oppression, is not located in a definition of socio-political systems (my apologies, Foucault, not only), but through felt oppression and an inability to relate, adhere and form a kinship - in other terms an arrest on a sense of belonging. If oppression or felt oppression exists, within a lived experience, one does not need to look up, down or all around - the system and processes that were implemented as preventative, safeguarding shield have failed and such a failure it is a miserable failure to human condition.

Belonging is defined in dictionary definitions as an affinity, a form of attachment, a bond to a situation or a place and clearly with a status of human relatedness.

Belonging is a powerful concept in psychotherapeutic and psychological interventions, a theoretical concept that can be applied across several protocols and in a myriad of formats. It can be about identity (identification), membership to a group, community, family, appertaining, adherence, self, relationships etc. But more so, it starts with being human.

I have made a clear choice about telling you, my readers, a story about (a) belonging - a subject, an object, a status, a concept, and an affinity: a history of its own, kind gestures, and a legacy of passing on an understanding. To my knowledge and practice-based understanding, belonging was about receiving a book review within a second-hand purchase from a book seller. I felt that I belong to that understanding, included in accessing and acting on someone's trust, gift, and ways of being. Perhaps being human starts with a sense of belonging if not being the beginning of existence itself.

I will never forget how hard I fought to find readings, books, classic manuscripts and how many gentle and kindred people were around me to facilitate and share such a passion. I am quite grateful to my neighbour that would lend me several of her hidden treasure books from before communist era, but equally I can recognise that within a democratic political system, much and many of similar oppressive practices are very much active. There is always a balance upon freedom of speech and disclosure on what one can term: infringements on () human rights. And that is when "belonging" or one's sense of belonging can be destabilized and subsequent questioning starts/: "Do I really want to be part of this?"

A simple recognition of infringement and violation is enough. The communists and militia had used subversive, covert operations in their forms of oppression and silencing anyone and everything that would stand against the regime. A democratic system that are using same processes, but formulated under different practices - it is absolutely no better than what it's so very well-known to I from my formative years. It was hard to watch burning of millions of books, to grow up with consciousness of what is prohibited to think, but it is harder, much harder, to live in a democratic society and see same processes at play with similar consequences, but politically decorated in demure statements of misunderstanding.

Belonging is a powerful concept, and its cultural implications are paramount. *A Memoir* by Willa Muir is magnificent, and I do recommend it.

I feel that July 2021 is a month of progress and moving on - in many a/ways that is also a form of belonging, for one to decide for themselves that it is time to move on and leave past to its past.

If you feel unsettled, in any measure, with a sense of self, please seek help, understanding is always on standby. That is a type of knowledge that matters most to human existence. There are many written reflections in *Belonging* that are highly relevant, one of my favourite one is on page 122 (hard copy) whereas Willa is preparing for second European adventure (1923 onwards), and declares:

"We were, it seems, turning into Europeans, after all..." (Muir, 122).

References:

Willa, M.(1968). *Belonging: a Memoir*. The Hogarth Press: London.

The Analyst: *There is a bounty on my head*

Chapter 6: An outreach psychotherapeutic service in South London

6.1. Case 1. Rhonda

What to keep in mind and the *order effect*

Disclosure statement: ***The below account is an example of study: Rhonda exists, all identifiers preserve patient's anonymous status, and confidentiality of "third" in the room.***

order effect

1. in within-subjects designs, the influence of the order in which treatments are administered, such as the effect of being the first administered treatment (rather than the second, third, and so forth). As individuals participate in first one and then another treatment condition, they may experience increased fatigue, boredom, and familiarity with or practice with reacting to the independent variable. Any of these conditions could affect the participants' responses and confound the results of the study. Researchers often use counterbalancing to control for order effects. See also carryover effect', sequence effect. (American Psychiatric Association, (APA) Dictionary of Psychology, 2021)

The above is a comprehensive definition and pertinent to specific knowledge - knowledge confined to psychology - mainstream - not so much to critical psychology: a counterpart that is assessing and reevaluating theoretical and scientific knowledge produced and qualified by various strands of psychology as a science based studies (evidence based) - the study of human behaviour - of socio-economic-political and human geography.

However, much can be applied and reapplied with such knowledge base, particularly when reintegrated in a different framework, that of psychosocial studies or even further but... There is a "But", nothing would matter more than stories/narratives of (a cumuli of) individual human experiences.

We are born humans and that is the very first definition and that is where and how Equality starts. We are all Man - Mankind - and minute of birth we are assigned to various categories, rights, labels, identifications, names, faith etc. - but nothing in future life prevents one to re/identify at any other point in life. Equality starts and exists with being a human - anything else after, or any next order qualification - it is an individual responsibility and a personal account of recognition. I am not suggesting that anything else is a choice, I am merely saying that Equality is not born out of fragmentation, but a choice and yes, indeed an order effect given at birth and for the duration of one's life. And I believe here is where *human effect* rather than *order effect* could intervene at any point in life. It is never too late in appropriating and understanding (or identifying) one sense of self. Everyone has a responsibility and accountability for that to happen.

Everyone has a right, human right to being them/self. I would go further than that and say, that by being human, everyone has a responsibility and accountability to being human as themselves, before identifying any other birth right or naming. Appropriation of every other identification comes with much accountability and responsibility.

There is always a choice. Always a choice including that of renouncing a birth right or identification or any other name category, for instance that of a nationality. That is something one can renounce or re/think in a course of life. Or any other type and or category part of a man made system of classification. That is not by being Radical but by being Fair to yourself. There are cases in the world, still, that by accumulating more than one or two ways of being - order effect - it is rather harmful to one self.

 I have one example in mind of dual nationality, still imprisoned and unable to free herself. That to me is enough to think that there is no higher authority, but that of HUMAN RIGHT to Exist therefore to decide for oneself rather than think there is something or someone out there that would come and save you. In a movie perhaps, but real life stories are what they are and that to me is evidence base knowledge. Identifying as a citizen or dual citizenship, more often than not, one is left with nothing other than themselves to Count and account. For them I speak.

What I had in mind for this month was a case study that I have been working on for over 14 years now. This month (May 2021) is the right time to publish it and publish it here. Or not. This case study is absolutely not disclosure, except for I working on it.

My order of identification remains as:

1. I am Human

2. I am Woman - and on this second identification I also say: *I am Mother.* It is my choice and it is about me. I was not always a Mother BUT always a Woman. I do not see that as fragmentation perhaps multiplication of same self-identified category. To me is important and that is my choice and my *Order Effect.* It was not always a choice, at least not before I actually experienced motherhood. Many could argue that same for Woman, except my body tells me different. I am not suggesting that Woman and Mother are interchangeable. I am just giving you an example as to how Order effect can work in real life without application of mainstream sample element. However, the second I say: I am a Mother - I also say: I am recognizing a system: an institution hence Mother to me is institutionalized. Same with saying: I am a Parent - I am not identifying a belonging to a group, but a System, hence again institutionalized. And same with any other identification including race, ethnicity and nationality or citizenship. All part of System not classifications, but Systems, and therefore institutionalized; this is my argument and it is based on years of study of lived experiences - not mine, but also mine.

Tomorrow, there is a BBC story on Medical Advances on Human Unborn Fetus. Today, I say that no advance in Medical practice is better or good enough for centuries of wrong doing, nevertheless, I do practice positivity and such positive aspects of saving one's life are remarkable for what they are. And still exclusive for what they are. Exclusive of any gratitude from me. Exclusive because when One suffers One is enough to also Count for All suffering. Consequences are funny things.

And so I return to completing 1 and 2, and say that it's enough for me to navigate my **_self-map,_** enough to understand and say: **I am. Differing perspectives are always going to be accepted.**

The Analyst: *There is a bounty on my head*

The case study that I had in mind it is a century old in its origin of study, it goes back to 1919-1920 and it concerns wearing a mask and a name: Joan Riviere. The mask that I speak of concerns a mask of knowledge, a mask of understanding how self-map is formed into the world. In this case study the mask stays always with the world - it is a *cultural understanding*, the *I* is formed by culture, politics, socio-economic status and human geography. It is never appropriated and when it becomes a self-identification that it's different from "normativity" or such exclusive understandings, the who/they are seen as deviating from the norm and experience violence - the type of violence that is unspeakable, unimaginable and (very) rarely talked about. That happens within the fragmentation of Being Human and self-identification beyond that. WOMAN's experiences are part of that story and sometimes such stories are part of or too within the mask - but unlike any other category Woman (is) not part of a System/ institutionalized - hence WOMAN's power and possibility.

Many will disagree and rightly so - everyone is entitled to a point of view - this space is not restricted - , but I claim WOMAN as *my second order category and see it as first order* - higher order or equal to I am Human=I am Woman. Anyone care to dismiss that?

Yes, many are and many will, but I am enough to stand for that. I am one and One is enough. I am not claiming belonging to a group, thus to have a second Woman by my side, but if anyone else aligns, are very welcomed.

My standpoint as Woman is enough for me to start building my understanding of the world around and see difference/ I will stay with **_human woman_** for the rest of my days. I am good with that. Joan Rivière (1929) seminal paper on female sexuality and "enigma" of "womanhood", what that may be, was interpreted by me as a turbulent time of finding new meanings, new ways to express an ephemeral reality:

"category of Woman/Women only needs Woman/Women to describe it and explain it to the world and not the other way around. That is the order effect. Each and every identification of self, makes up self. There is a choice.

Always a choice". (Day, 1973)

The Analyst: *There is a bounty on my head*

1. *I* am Human;

2. *I* am Woman;

Or I am a Woman and Human or I am Woman.

Anyone can say I am...

and then finding their way to what next.

References:

Dictionary.apa.org. 2021. APA Dictionary of Psychology. [online] Available at: [Accessed 20 February 2021]

Rivière, J.(1929). "Womanliness as a masquerade". *International Journal of Psycho-Analysis.* Vol 9. Pp. 303-313.

The Analyst: *There is a bounty on my head*

6.2. Case 2. Hassan

A case of climbing the tree/therapy - Hassan

Disclosure statement: ***The below account is an example of study: Hassan exists, all identifiers preserve patient's anonymous status, and confidentiality of "third" in the room.***

Here's what we've been working on

I had in mind so much more for October 2021 and in many ways that is exactly how things have progressed - not what I have planned for - meaning that I had a clear set of ideas in transcribing existing **interviews** on links between mental health and nutrition and creating an interview schedule with similar questions to a wider expert audience.

So, October 2021 is now about a wonderful article that I've published with *Counselling Directory* on the 14th of September 2021

and here is the September 21/October 21 article:

"Having therapy is climbing a tree?"

By Madalina Day dedicated to Hassan

Published on 14th September, 2021

No, therapy is wanting to climb a tree!

"I am looking through some of the photos from Royal Academy of Arts (RA) for this month, especially the ones marketed on social media. One such image captured my attention; I did not look quite so closely, I did not read all the subtitles, the image was speaking to me – it seemed like tree trunks neatly arranged one next to each other, reaching for the sky in a perfect circular position and with light climbing down from a ground perspective rather than from a top view.

The Analyst: *There is a bounty on my head*

Images are powerful to my attentiveness and perception and so, I started to rethink a way out from that image: how would I climb out and towards the light? No idea, really, at that very moment. I was much more preoccupied by contemplating the image: its beauty, perfections, monochromatic sense and feelings entrapped in that circular movement with tree trunks reaching for the sky and the eye viewer trapped into that sense of space constructed in such a way. I immediately wondered: was that the intention of the artist? To place herself/himself/themselves in such a position and point of view – something to aspire and inspire without immediately seeking a way out? It would make sense, it is art – speaks to us all in such different ways. I was uncertain and that is how that image was making me feel. I felt that it would feel safer, if perhaps there was a sense of urgency to climb out and towards the light. What other options were there? And then the most peculiar thing happened. The image changed its conceptual feeling of entrapment into a memory of climbing a tree as a young child – that made me feel curious and excited. I wanted to climb out. I was ready to climb out. I wanted to reach out and I looked forward to finding such ways out. The trees' trunks were my friends, my stairs out into the light and then my vision and my mind would climb out of that ground circle and into the light. I was not thinking about the artist anymore, I was now finding a way out, but also remembering that I am curious and not afraid, I am engaged and not pressured, I am present and focused and not feeling lost or doubtful of a sense of what next: I felt that I had a purpose.

All the above are about ways of engaging in therapy - all such ways presented in metaphorical ways and not attempting to dismiss or remodel therapy as not being a treatment for mental health issues. On the contrary – it opens something that so many of us, practitioners, think about and face on a day-to-day basis in our practice. Yes, therapeutic interventions are protocols designed for and targeting mental health and that are indisputable facts. But that is not all that there is.

Therapy and its interventions (in whatever modality or school of thought) are also human ways to self-discover, to self-learn about self and the world at large, a way of relating or finding an anchor in your life, and also particularly when one herself/himself/themselves offer such ways to others. Therapeutic interventions can also be treated as courses of training in self-development and understanding, and as such I have listed the below for ways of thinking about therapy.

The Analyst: *There is a bounty on my head*

It may feel like this article goes against the tide of thinking about therapy as a course of action for distress and alleviating suffering - again, indisputable facts; yes, absolutely therapy is a space where the unbearable moments of day-to-day, minute to minute of a life overwhelmed by one or two or more mental health issues or of an emotional life filled with grief and or bereavement can take place – yes, therapy responds and attends to that, too. Therapeutic interventions are designed, protocols are named and formulated around clinical diagnosis of painful mental health conditions.

As a practitioner, I acknowledge that clinical depression and despondent feelings are a dark state of mind, I acknowledge that anxiety disorders exist in different degrees, I acknowledge and attest that I have met and treated dissociative and personality disorders of all types, degrees and severity; there is no condition recognised in either DSM-V or ICD-11 that I have not treated as a practitioner of mental health or recognised as being assigned in such category/classification. Yes, I acknowledge that phobias are real, PTSD is treatable, and abnormality takes different meanings when placed within a clinical psychology terrain. Yes, I am aware of panic disorder and its many forms, but then again, I also know that therapeutic interventions or therapeutic encounters are also about:

1. Helping and supporting the patient to become curious – really and mostly at its core – that is exactly what therapy it's all about. I do hope that my statement is not provoking any disconcerting feelings on part of readers.

2. Helping and supporting the patient to want to know.

3. Helping and supporting the patient to find her/his/their way out.

4. Helping and supporting the patient to climb a tree or remembering the first time they did so.

5. Helping and supporting the patient to see/envisage their future.

6. Helping and supporting the patient to write up or think on their goals/purpose.

7. Helping and supporting the patient through difficult psychological transitions/changes/life events.

Therapy need not be painful – today offers different challenges to what was such a long time ago seen as a "mental disturbance". That is the stereotype and that needs to be eliminated. Therapy is real, as real as its needs and outreach.

Therapy can be a method of training, training your sense of self, nourishing and healing, but also self-growth.

Therapy can be many things, but more importantly it can be what you wish it for. Remember that! "

References:

Day, M. (2023)., *Letter to Hassan was overdue*. New Beginnings Therapy: London.

Light Lines: The Architectural Photographs of Hélène Binet | Exhibition | Royal Academy of Arts, 2021

The Analyst: *There is a bounty on my head*

Chapter 7: Association of Analysis and Psychotherapy Public and Private Service in North-East London

7.1.Case 1. Samantha

Letter to the editors of "Therapy Today" (TT) publication: *Why writing is of essence in Psychotherapy even when you get it wrong. 2017/January*

Disclosure statement: *The below account is an example of study: Samantha exists, all identifiers preserve patient's anonymous status, and confidentiality of "third" in the room.*

In the last year or so I've submitted couple of pieces of writing to the "Therapy Today"(TT) editorial team. All proposals were rejected for various reasons and, ultimately, part-letter is published below:

The feedback, on the last response, made me realise that I am writing with no desire to be published by TT, but from a desire to communicate what I know of my profession, my professional experience, and what I see as a method of communication amongst many of my peers. Lately, and when reading TT, I feel less and less connected with a wider group of therapists/psychotherapists - I do identify personal experiences and various specific places of practice - the client group is less prevalent as a topic – in one of TT's recent publication there was a subject topic on what practice means in terms of providing a therapeutic service to millennials. Another monthly publication mentioned, in more general terms, how we tackle race in counselling and psychotherapeutic professions; all really welcomed and somehow potentially informative topics (demographics not on its own) to professionals engaged in practice of psychotherapy and/or counselling. I have not yet managed to find that point of connectiveness between my views on various perspectives, i.e. geopolitical, economic and social (en)culturation, as a supposed topic matter for TT magazine. I do, however, recall reading it as early as 00s, and perhaps it just made me feel as if a categorical change on part of TT took place in the last decades.

Today, that realisation, of my wish to communicate and find points of reference with other professionals ON Ethics, felt increasingly stronger - a very clear and *visible topic. I believe that my thinking of TT as a forum for counselling and psychotherapeutic professions was mistaken. It is not a research journal, and my interests are very much about finding a connection with <u>progressive thinking, change and applied practice.</u>*

To my question as to why writing is important for analysts, well, it is my intact belief that communication is representative of my profession, and writing on topics of interest arrived at from practice, proposing such topics to other peer professionals, is an integral part of who I am. Analysts are writers by the very nature of their being – not because that is what they've signed up on when starting a career in therapeutic professions and/or psychoanalytical professions, but it is in writing that an individual is committed to that very profession. An analyst is a writer and vice versa, may also be true. It comes with the job description of communication. An active communicator and advocate for their profession, hence self-denomination - a psychoanalyst in my case. And, yes, editorial teams can decide on type and/or topics of their content, but, and then again, if I am going to read promoted published work with no original writings or real practice reflections as aspects of day-in work, PERHAPS IT IS NOT I THAT NEED A RETHINK ON ETHICS AND STANDARDS; also, possible that perhaps I have just outgrown "TT" for what it currently stands. What do YOU think? The gatekeepers of all professions are professionals in practice, and my feel is that TT is mostly about promoting an administrative body that represents a cumulative of secretarial jobs and nothing to do with clinical work. And part of intended letter is now published. I wish I had a few extra notes on the above letter including newly acquired views, truth be told, there is a repeated observation : "violence against difference and representatives of standpoint theory is real, and it can manifest in most absurd ways." History is there to be analysed and, when time comes, also enabling a move forward from such organisations, individuals and/or matters of harm.

To I, healing comes from self-acknowledgment and self-belief.

The Analyst: *There is a bounty on my head*

7.2.Case 2. Elvin

Memory and reflective practice - why are important for a successful therapeutic encounter

Disclosure statement: ***The below account is an example of study: Elvin exists, all identifiers preserve patient's anonymous status, and confidentiality of "third" in the room.***

Memory and reflective practice - why are important for a successful therapeutic encounter

One of my favourite best scholars of all times is Judith Butler - for all of their writings, interpretative readings, texts, in-person conferences etc., over a period of more than twenty years.

One of the best aspects of Butler's writings (in my opinion) is that they and their' readings are not immediately conquering a conceptual understanding. Allow me an example: Butler's quote in a chapter entitled "*Against Ethical Violence*" in their book "*Giving an Account of Oneself*" (2005) is significant to title of my this subchapter; Butler contends:

" *Consider that one way we become responsible and self-knowing is facilitated by a kind of reflection that takes place when judgment is suspended. Condemnation, denunciation, and excoriation work as quick ways to posit an ontological difference between judge and judged, even to purge oneself of another. Condemnation becomes the way in which we establish the other as unrecognizable or jetti-son some aspect of ourselves that we lodge in the other, whom we then condemn. In this sense, condemnation can work against self-knowledge, inasmuch as it moralizes a self by disavowing commonality with the judged. Although self-knowledge is surely limited, that is not a reason (enough.sic.. my own addition to text) to turn against it as a project. Condemnation tends to do precisely this, to purge and externalize one's own opacity. In this sense, judgment can be a way to fail to own one's limitations and thus provide no felicitous basis for a reciprocal recognition of human beings as opaque to themselves, partially blind, constitutively limited. To know oneself as limited is still to know something about oneself, even if one's knowing is afflicted by the limitation that one knows.*

The Analyst: *There is a bounty on my head*

Similarly, condemnation is very often an act that not only "gives up on" the one condemned but seeks to inflict a violence upon the condemned in the name of "ethics". Butler, 2005,p.46.

A brief illustration of my own understanding/meaning of ethical violence of my account with an object (rather) than a subject:

The object in question is actually a KNIFE. In each and every culture - knives - have a purpose, a meaning - a collective understanding. I shall acknowledge all such meanings and tell you my relationship with a knife:

1. As a child I used a knife to sharpen my pencils for obvious purposes - writing - I never had a pencil sharpener during my formative years.

2. I also used knives as a tool in the kitchen - for its purposes as a cutlery utensil and for cooking, chopping etc.

3. I very often use a knife as a tool to fix things, remove or cut something, when I can't find something as a proper tool i.e. replacing a fuse or opening a tin can.

4. Camping - any form of knife* is a must for survival - one can decide and identify for themselves ways of usage.

5. Carving, sculpting etc. - it is probably not called knife* - but all along it is its purpose - remodelling, changing, altering to a form that can be best sharp in its entirety.

6. but KNIFE has a major meaning, linked to both self-defences and aggression/violence - it is a symbol for all that can be conceptualised as survival - its existence is designed for survival in all its forms. It is classified as a *white weapon* or *cold weapon* - defined as "a weapon that does not involve fire or explosions, weapons that do not use any sort of explosive force in their function" *Wikipedia cold weapon.*

I often think at that association and think back at Butler's quote - I think my weapon of choice is sharpening my pencils, like I did as a child. However, I

recognise that my pencil is now a knife itself, and it can be used in all potential 1 to 6 of above. My pencil is a

KNIFE itself in both purpose and usage. Probably not quite so obvious at first look, but from capability vantage point absolutely so. As it would be if I refer to a chopstick. Coming back to writings of *condemned* - KNIFE- it is condemned and restricted in its limits for its own declaration of purpose knowledge - and yet, knives are objects and "subjects" indisputably representing a survival.

I will go back and sharpen my pencils, or wait,... now I can just type: my fingers are my knife, absorbed into my skin, my being - my very memory, hence used *against ethical violence*, talking about my taking a stand against violence - ethical violence in all its forms. Every word of mine, can be equally a knife's stab and/or a soothing thought. That is a choice - can it be both? Interpretatively?

It depends. Depends on what one identifies as main and only usage of a KNIFE. Does one identify oneself as a feeder, carver, acting in self-defence, fixing things, enabling an understanding or randomly acting purposely to attack someone through sharpening of pencils and purport ethical violence in the name of condemnation? Clear distinctions above - use your knives carefully and when you, yourself become a knife make choices against violence - put your cold weapon down and only resort to such defence when it is ultimate. As a child, I did not have a pencil sharpener - but I did make sure that my own child had one such object from each and every place of art that we have visited, with name and purpose clearly defined. If you are still wondering on psychotherapeutic meanings on all above, please create a list of your own usage of a knife and meanings attached. Read that list again and reflect on previously accepted understandings. I hope you would not have to challenge yourself and that all is clear on your side. But, is it? Clear?

References:

Butler, J., (2005)., *Giving an account of oneself*. New York: Fordham University Press.

The Analyst: *There is a bounty on my head*

Chapter 8: Private practice therapeutic services London

8.1.Case 1. Rea

Rea: Creativity and *safe places* in therapy

Disclosure statement: ***The below account is an example of study: Rea exists, all identifiers preserve patient's anonymous status, and confidentiality of "third" in the room.***

Creativity and *safe places* in therapy

One of the most basic rule in psychotherapy, specifically employed when practicing breathing exercises and mindfulness it's that of holding a safe space for content and imaginary exploration; a process of , enabling, guiding and holding a confidential place where clients can develop and examine their inner worlds and imaginary safe places.

Breathing exercises and mindfulness in therapy are very much part of a client's inner dialogue that then is canvased onto a dialogue and communication with their therapist – the client/patient can create such images with their mind, exploring their aims and creating a safe place that can be reached when feeling overwhelmed and or distressed one way or another.

Colour and choice of colours are essential in breathing exercises and various forms of meditation and in therapy clients are encouraged to describe their emotional understanding of different colours and attach their own personal meanings. However that is not to say that colours in emotional terms are universal because that is really not the case but what matters most is whether or not there is harmony, connectedness and creating that emotional content whatever that may be

Mind and body alignment and or emotional connectedness - it may sound as .most encountered phrases for desired states of being, certainly some of the most sought after in therapeutic encounters and described as seeking restfulness, peacefulness and inner peace. In many instances, such meditative states are simply about readiness for day/s ahead, a very well established practice as daily routine and a timeout from a rapid - or what it's felt as rapid - pace of daily life. One central premise when practicing breathing exercises with clients/patients is based around ideas of **acceptance.**

Acceptance is not for things that can be changed, but for things that cannot be changed - we can alleviate, address, enable, empower, live in, gain insight and all with (self) compassion and a wish for healing. There are situations when such practices are integrated into a larger focus for client's work as forms of explorations and healing psychological/emotional wounds.

There are states of being that form part of who we are and in such states, restlessness and or a racing mind are the very ways of being that then need negotiating and peacefully asserted and guided **to ways of coexisting with requirements of realities of our lives.**

Another version of above thoughts was also provided to Counselling Directory for a wider reach to interested public with a recognition of aspects discussed being of importance to wellbeing of population at large.

Recent research on emotions and colours presents interesting findings and cross cultural differences (geographical proximity and linguistics); for any curious reader about this topic, an interesting read can be found here:
https://journals.sagepub.com/doi/10.1177/0956797620948810

References:

Colour and choice of colours are essential in breathing exercises and various forms of meditation and in therapy clients are encouraged to describe their emotional understanding of different colours and attach their own personal meanings. However that is not to say that colours in emotional terms are universal because that is really not the case, but what matters most is whether or not there is harmony, connectedness and creating that emotional content whatever that may be. (Day, 2022)

The Analyst: *There is a bounty on my head*

8.2.Case 2. Harley

A case of rules: Standards and Values or Values and Standards

Therapeutic Relationship

Disclosure statement: *The below account is an example of study: Harley exists, all identifiers preserve patient's anonymous status, and confidentiality of "third" in the room.*

How can counselling/ psychotherapy help?

And now, imagine opening your front door to a day that is absorbing clear blue skies and you starting your journey into your moments with confidence about navigating your next, and when and if necessary, allowing stillness and peacefulness to pass your way. Imagine the most ordinary day of your life to be exciting, with a you bearably attending to your day, your future and making the most of your relationship with significant others. Imagine a day where a journey into work feels only one step away from you achieving your dreams and that journey back home when there is an acute sense of "I can do this!" Imagine what it is like to think that having a *bad day* is OK and readjust your expectations of self, others and the world to realistic and specific hopes without being self-critical and envisaging a better rather than a lesser. A client told me, not so long ago, that therapy helped her shift her perspective with starting thinking of the world as being potential and achieving an optimistic sense of self. She became able to work through her difficulties and thinking on opportunities, but most importantly she stopped counting her *bad days*. Her feedback remained with me as the most insightful way of looking at a therapeutic encounter as an encounter that accounts for both the therapeutic process and the outcome.

I practice a type of therapy that is guided by my clients, where I offer experience, skills and understanding that are specifically designed as steps to exploration, examination and hopefully, culminating with clients acquiring an understanding of self and experiences that are translated in everyday life moments.

My practice of Counselling/Psychotherapy is seen as mediated through a rapport, working alliance or a therapeutic relationship where the client is encouraged, engaged and guided whilst guiding his/her counsellor/psychotherapist through such a process. In long term psychodynamic therapy such understandings are seen as reaching deeply into unconscious processes that are then, through therapeutic interventions, dynamically brought up to the surface of consciousness and, if possible, resolved. If a brief psychodynamic therapy is suitable, we agree on a number of sessions six or twelve - depending on the nature of your difficulties - and time-limited work planned, focussed and agreed at the beginning of your therapeutic contract. If Cognitive Behavioural Therapy is most appropriate to your presenting situation we will aim to attend to your thoughts, behaviours and emotions, bringing clarity to your days.

I do not promise impossible, I do not practice a therapy that would solve your problems, I do not offer advice, I shall not know your solutions, but I do commit to a statement that if it feels difficult there is a chance for change and that there are possibilities through a therapeutic process for change to be achieved. I do adhere and practice in accordance to therapeutic principles and approaches that would prove valuable to you to gain an insight in your difficulties and find solutions to your problems. I shall not be alone in such a quest, my experience and skills are clinically supervised, I am a practitioner with adherence to Ethical Guidelines of Good Practice and I practice with a commitment to continuous personal development to the best interest of my clients.

Chapter 9: Private practice analysis and psychotherapy word-wide

Case 1. Dan

A case of acute sleeping and 5S strategy: Dan

Disclosure statement: ***The below account is an example of study: Dan exists, all identifiers preserve patient's anonymous status, and confidentiality of "third" in the room.***

 First moment of everyday, or first moment of waking-up, I called it a memory*. That is a choice, my choice based on my experience, it is also a choice based on research - not only from its references, but so much more. This blog is not proposing a debate on its topic, but rather aims to prompt a (self) reflection.

What is your first awake moment like? Is it similar every day? If so, why would that be?

Most articles in below list are free to access, some have a shareable link next to its reference. Hope it helps!

<u>The meaning of space: 5Ss Strategy developed and researched by Dr. Madalina Day (2019)</u>

"There are numerous leaflets and strategies on sleep that I have come across on my journey to become a counsellor/psychotherapist, and what I have come to realise is that one important aspect in the assessment of our distress is a capacity to identify the source of difficulty, in relation to everything else that we represent. That being said, counselling and/or psychotherapy is one such point of contact for guidance and relational help.

5 Points of strategy to develop a healthy sleep schedule was constructed as a 5S's strategy.

The Analyst: *There is a bounty on my head*

I have designed the five steps to nurturing a healthy sleep schedule, to help you explore and relate to your sleeping environment; the five S's could be simply conceptualised as a visualisation technique.

S1: Stands for SPACE

Like with anything, every person would have a designated space to rest. That is to say that nighttime would involve a routine, and for that to happen in connection to sleep, one would first need to identify that space. If you do have trouble sleeping and/or difficulties getting to sleep, the first thing you should do differently is to recognise and reassign your space and setting for sleep. And to reassign does not necessarily imply you need to change your sleep environment, but perhaps rethink it and try and see it as new.

S2: Stands for SCHEDULE

Acknowledging and assigning a specific time as part of your routine for sleep is one other important aspect of a healthy sleep schedule. There are times in our lives when certain actions and or basic needs become increasingly challenging.

When our sleep pattern is changing, quality of sleep and its duration are some of the factors that give us an indication of such changes. Allocating a specific time and scheduling a set time for sleep (e.g. 9 pm switch off electronics, 10 pm means bedtime) would enable you to actively intervene in your sleep pattern and modify it to your assessed needs.

S3: Stands for SLOWING DOWN

After the first two aspects of your sleep schedule are identified and agreed, slowing down as part of this routine is your next step every night. Slowing down means that you are synchronising your body and mind and prepare yourself for your night sleep.

The Analyst: *There is a bounty on my head*

There are several ways of achieving this and it depends on your own meaning of "slowing down". Generally, slowing down is an attribution to actions and/or a state of mind before your scheduled time with sleep. It could be that you decide to read a book or go out for a night walk. It's a preparatory step where you detach from daily preoccupations and commence your new sleep pattern to a chosen schedule.

S4: Stands for SENSES

As you are in your chosen sleep environment at your scheduled sleep time after slowing down, your next step is to channel your mind on your senses:

- **Sensation:** your sleep environment becomes a place where your body is immersing, leaving behind daily tensions, with your breathing adjusting to calmness in your body.

- **Sight:** eyes closed, bringing images to mind that are aligned to the calmness of your body, memories of happy times or creating new places in corners of your mind associated with sleep.

- **Sound:** peaceful sounds depending on your selected images.

- **Smell:** what is it like to be there?

- **Taste:** what place is imagined and what association/s could be made? Is it being at an imagined seaside, tasting the saltiness of a soft breeze?

5S: Stands for SAVE AS

This final step is adding an element to the previous four steps and, if necessary, a repetition of step 4. With all in mind, a sense of safety is added, where a feeling of embracing and welcoming your new sleep routine is acknowledged as a planned and vital part of who you are.

In this sense, sleep and a healthy sleep routine are reconstructed as an essential part of you - its importance is reconsidered and not treated as a challenge, but as a re-attribution of your meanings. During this final step, you are ascertaining to yourself your new sleep routine with perseverance and consistency."

References:

Aston-Jones, G. (2005) "Brain structures and receptors involved in alertness," *Sleep Medicine*, 6. Available at: https://doi.org/10.1016/s1389-9457(05)80002-4.

Day, M. (2019.) "*The meaning of space: Sleep and functional well-being*", *Counselling Directory*. Available at: https://www.counselling-directory.org.uk/memberarticles/on-sleep-and-functional-well-being-the-meaning-of-space (Accessed: March 24, 2023).

Ellington, D. (....) *There's a paper bird in my heart... all of my own...*, Darcy Ellington. Tumblr. Available at: https://darcyellington.tumblr.com/post/181986860585/theres-a-paper-bird-in-my-heart-all-of-my-own/amp (Accessed: March 24, 2023).

Ehlers, C.L. et al. (1998) "The Pittsburgh Study of normal sleep in young adults: Focus on the relationship between waking and sleeping EEG spectral patterns," *Electroencephalography and Clinical Neurophysiology*, 106(3), pp. 199–205. Available at: https://doi.org/10.1016/s0013-4694(97)00130-2.

Goldman-Schuyler, K. et al. (2016) "'Moments of waking up": A doorway to mindfulness and presence," *Journal of Management Inquiry*, 26(1), pp. 86–100. Available at: https://doi.org/10.1177/1056492616665171 - free article

Making peace with the first moment of the day (2017) Raptitude.com. Available at: https://www.raptitude.com/2017/11/making-peace-with-the-first-moment-of-the-day/ (Accessed: March 24, 2023).

Sanders, R. (2022) Scientists discover secret to waking up alert and refreshed, Berkeley News. Available at: https://news.berkeley.edu/2022/11/29/scientists-discover-secret-to-waking-up-alert-and-refreshed/ (Accessed: March 24, 2023).

Special issue: Memory and desire - reading Freud (2006) BPS. The British Psychological Society. Available at: https://www.bps.org.uk/psychologist/special-issue-memory-and-desire-reading-freud(Accessed: March 24, 2023).

Tahmasian, M. et al. (2020) "The interrelation of sleep and mental and physical health is anchored in grey-matter neuroanatomy and under genetic control," *Communications Biology*, 3(1). Available at: https://doi.org/10.1038/s42003-020-0892-6.

University of Copenhagen - The Faculty of Health and Medical Sciences. (2022, July 14). "Stress transmitter wakes your brain more than 100 times a night -- and it is perfectly normal." *ScienceDaily.* Retrieved March 21, 2023 from www.sciencedaily.com/releases/2022/07/220714103016.htm

Vallat, R., Berry, S.E., Tsereteli, N. et al. "How people wake up is associated with previous night's sleep together with physical activity and food intake". *Nature Communications.* 13, 7116 (2022). https://doi.org/10.1038/s41467-022-34503-2. (share link: https://rdcu.be/c8nck Provided by the Springer Nature SharedIt content-sharing initiative)

The Analyst: *There is a bounty on my head*

Case 2. Aola

Debating psychopathology – A research case

Disclosure statement: *The below account is an example of study: Aola exists, all identifiers preserve patient's anonymous status, and confidentiality of "third" in the room.*

This subchapter is proposing a succinct critical evaluation of existing research literature on psychopathology and, more specifically, is going to critically analyse definitional associations between psychopathy and criminality, biological basis for psychopathy, similarities and differences between psychopathic personality and antisocial personality disorder and current developments in assessment of psychopathy. This review is structured in three parts, each such part representing various degrees of understanding and associated research evidence for the aforementioned considerations.

Definitions and classification of psychopathy are presented and linked to current research on criminality. This part is also going to attempt a clear response to the proposed statement that psychopaths are unable to prevent themselves from acting anti-socially, assess various features of psychopathy and its link to genetic predispositions of psychopaths and their anti-social behaviour. The second part of this paper is going to focus on biological basis for psychopathy, evaluate recent scientific findings and its implication for distinguishing between possible psychopathic subtypes such as primary and secondary psychopathy (Huss, 2014). The third and last section of this analysis is an evaluation of assessment of psychopathy and recent developments in the field. Such considerations are offered as an attempt to bring to the fore scientific evidence in order to inform initial stages of decision making in public policy regarding a proposed bill that would require pre-emptive indefinite hospitalization in a secure facility for psychopaths. A summary of findings is going to form the conclusion of this paper. The outcome is accompanied by a suggested acknowledgement that all findings need to be viewed alongside issues of ethics and methodology and not in isolation. All such analysis was developed as part of a reflective practice between February 2018 and March 2019.

The Analyst: *There is a bounty on my head*

By way of introduction and in consideration of the first two statements proposed for analysis, a) psychopaths are criminal by definition and b) individuals with psychopathy are unable to prevent themselves from acting anti-socially, the nature of psychopathy and its classification with the psychological realms are necessary.

Cleckely (1941) offered one of the most used modern conception of psychopathy. Cleckley (1976) identified 16 different characteristics encompassed in a clinical profile of the psychopath. It included: a superficial charm and good intelligence, unreliability, lack of remorse and or shame, poor judgment and failure to learn from experience, incapacity for love and a general unresponsiveness in affective interpersonal relations (Huss, 2014). All such characteristics were identified during a trial in the UK during 2017/2018. Cleckley's work on psychopathy influenced and inspired both early research on psychopathy and classification of behaviour in 2nd edition of the Diagnostic and Statistical Manual of Mental Disorders DSM- II (Skeem et al. 2011). Such influence has continued and considerations of Cleckley's work is reflected in revised editions of DSM and its European counterpart classification, that of International Statistical Classification of Diseases and Related Health Problems – ICD. According to the revised Diagnostic and Statistical Manual of Mental Disorders (DSM-V; American Psychiatric Association, 2013), psychopathy can be construed as a clinical form of personality disorder and more specifically that of Antisocial Personality Disorder (Antisocial PD). In the tenth edition of International Statistical Classification of Diseases and Mental Health (ICD -10), published by World Health Organisation (WHO), psychopathy is closely linked to Dissocial Personality Disorder (Dissocial PD). In ICD-10 Dissocial PD is defined as a condition characterised by a disregard for social obligations, and callous unconcern for the feelings of others (F60.2, WHO. 1990). All such disregards for social obligation being well documented in various documents available to all agencies involved in the aforementioned Court Case on the applicant father. The cluster of features in Dissocial PD present a distinct and clear disparity between behaviour and the prevailing social norms, but more importantly suggest that behaviour cannot be easily altered by adverse experience including previous punishment. In this regard, it can be said that individuals diagnosed with Dissocial PD cannot prevent themselves from acting antisocial. Nevertheless, the criteria, albeit focused on affective deficits, cannot be found as representative of the overall behavioural and personality traits present in psychopathy (Ogloff, 2006) and in that sense, such understandings cannot be extended to psychopathy. The same observations are pertinent to the DSM – IV – TR criteria for antisocial personality disorder, although it is recognised that more emphasis is placed on common antisocial components of behaviour between PD and generalised psychopathy. In DSM – IV – TR, Antisocial Personality Disorder is described as: a pervasive pattern of disregard for and violation of the rights of others occurring since age 15 years, as indicated by three (or more) of the following:

1.Failure to confirm to social norms with respect to lawful behaviours as indicated by repeatedly performing acts that are grounds for arrest.

2.Deceitfulness, as indicated by repeated lying, use of aliases, or conning others for personal profit and pleasure.

3.Impulsivity and failure to plan ahead

4.Irritability and aggressiveness

5.Reckless disregard for safety of self or others

6.Consistent irresponsibility

7.Lack of remorse

DSM IV and V states that Antisocial PD had also been referred to as psychopathy, sociopathy, or dissocial personality disorder.

Returning to psychopathology, a discriminatory act, the suggested collapse of terms has generated a reasonable amount of discussion at both theoretical level and amongst clinicians (Hare & Neumann, 2009), but more importantly has highlighted the cautiousness that needs to be employed when assessing statements such as psychopaths are by definition criminals. As it can be seen, psychopathy as a concept is highly problematic and incredibly difficult to disentangle from either antisocial behaviour and or affective deficits. Nevertheless, research on psychopathy has been seen as closely related to such constructs and equally different in that of including a distinct cluster of interpersonal, affective, lifestyle and antisocial traits and behaviours (Hare & Neumann, 2009). At an interpersonal level, individuals with psychopathy have been described as deceptive, dominant, superficial, grandiose and manipulative. Affectively, it is found that one important aspect of psychopathy concerns the inability to form and maintain strong attachment and/or relational bonds with others, coupled with a lack of empathy, guilt and remorse (Schimmenti et al, 2014).

Considering criteria present in both APD and Dissocial PD it is relatively clear as to why psychopathy as a clinical construct can be associated with both classifications of personality disorders and tied to a socially deviant lifestyle, however, such irresponsible and impulsive behaviour are seen as not necessarily criminal in nature (Hare & Neumann, 2013). Moreover, owed to such clinical understandings that psychopaths exhibit interpersonal emotional and cognitive deficits, various studies have further explored the biological basis for psychopathy in looking at both genetic factors and neurobiological evidence (Huss, 2014). What has been found is that a common genetic factor could account for significant variance across all four psychopathy factors (Hare and Neumann, 2009). Several twin studies comparing both identical and fraternal twins have yielded similar results, supporting the statement that psychopathy is a condition with strong genetic basis (Pozzulo et. al., 2013). A study by Bloningen, Carlson, Kruger, and Patrick (2003) with adult male twin pairs participants – 165 monozygotic (MZ) and 106 dizygotic (DZ) - and examining the etiology of psychopathy using a personality approach, revealed a substantial genetic influence. The authors' findings were compatible with previously reported evidence regarding both antisocial and criminal behaviour (Bloningen at. Al 2003). In another study by Bloningen, Hicks, Kruger, Patrick and Iacono (2005), twin analyses suggested a significant genetic influence on distinct psychopathic traits such as fearless dominance and impulsive antisociality. Furthermore, it was found that fearless dominance was associated with reduced genetic risk for internalising psychopathology, whereas impulsive antisociality was associated with increased genetic risk for externalising psychopathology (Bloningen et. al. 2005). The latter association being highly significant to subsequent accounts on psychopathy as a construct and further debates on how psychopathy at theoretical and measurable level is distinct from both antisocial behaviour and criminal behaviour. Hart et al (1990) administered a variety of neuropsychological tests to two sample of participants divided in low, medium and high psychopathy. Their findings suggest that there criminal psychopaths did not differ from other criminals in their performance. More importantly, the test scores of all participants, as well as global ratings of impairment, were not significantly different from those typically obtained with non-criminals of approximately similar age and education (Hart et. al. 1990). A recent study, Motzkin, et al. 2001 considers that various functional brain structures such as amygdala and the prefrontal cortex are relevant and involved in psychopathy and distinguishing between psychopathic subtypes, such as low anxious/ primary psychopathy and high anxious/ secondary psychopathy) , is crucial to clarifying the neural correlates of psychopathy. Such studies although can account for a significant genetic influence present across psychopathy domains, do not reject the possibility that environmental factors can and do part-take, influencing how these innate traits are expressed.

What is yet to be clarified is a thorough understanding on the centrality of criminal lifestyle to the concept of **psychopathy**. From what has been attended to so far, a clear association between criminality and psychopathy is apparent, however, there is a clear need for clarification as to what type of association that is: whether criminality is highly correlated to psychopathy or it's simply a core feature of a clinical profile of a psychopath. Skeem and Cooke (2010) pose a similar question in assessing an essence of psychopathy. Both researchers define criminal behaviour as distinct from antisocial behaviour, inclusive of criminal behaviour that extends beyond markers of adult development including criminal behaviour in early development. The two investigators, further argue that criminal behaviour lies within a conceptual domain strictly defined as violation of legal rules and what constitutes a law system whereas personality deviation is reflective of a violation of interpersonal norms, hence the collapsed understandings should not be equated. Skeem and Cooke (2010) suggests that although it can be recognised that specific personality traits are inferred across various contexts with some traits of psychopathic personality also identifiable as behaviour that defeats social order, it would be conceptually flowed if indicators of psychopathic traits are fixed on criminal acts. In making such conceptual and linear differences, Skeem and Cooke (2010) are overtly critical of the work of Hare and Newman (2005) that, according to Skeem and Cooke's interpretation, are scholars that consider antisocial behaviour critical and central to psychopathy and where criminal behaviour is a prominent feature of antisocial behaviour (Skeem and Cooke, 2010). Moreover, Skeem and Cooke's (2010) question the widely used Psychopathy Checklist - Revised (PCL –R) a measure of psychopathy devised by Robert Hare, in that of being highly problematic as it equates a structure of a construct with a model of psychopathy. Nevertheless, the PCL –R has been developed to measure the extent to which an individual meets the criteria for psychopathy in all four domains, and as such provides a score to which an individual presents characteristics consistent with psychopathy. The PCL-R is composed of 20 items and divided in two groups. Because the PCL-R is scored from 0 to 2, scores range from 0 to 40 and a score of 30 and greater is considered conservative score for psychopathy (Huss, 2014). Although the PCL-R cut-off score of 30 has proven essential in research and applications and understanding of psychopathy, some investigators have used other cut-offs scores for psychopathy: as score of 25 in some European studies (Hare and Neumann, 2009). It is generally agreed that PCL-R scores in the upper-range (30 and higher) are reflective across population sample of psychopathy in North-American male offenders as they do in female offenders and European male offenders and forensic psychiatric patients (Hare and Neumann, 2009). In response to Skeem and Cooke's (2010) article, Hare and Neumann (2010) consider that Skeem and Cooke (2010) offered a simplistic understanding of psychopathy using a two factor model and in offering a critique of Hare and Neumann's (2005) work in relation to the essence of psychopathy, they themselves failed to distinguish between the antisocial behaviour and criminal behaviour, using the two constructs interchangeably. Hare and Neumann (2010) state that, if indeed, academics or readers of Skeem and Cooke's (2010) article are to correctly conceive their argument about the centrality of criminality to psychopathy, the reader should replace the word criminality with antisociality.

To conclude, what is fundamental to note is that associations between psychopathy and criminality and psychopathy and antisocial behaviour is extremely complex and by a careful consideration of such constructs, prominent experts and researchers in the field are further complicating current understandings in creating conceptual barriers. Collapsing terms such as criminal and antisocial behaviour or incorporating such terms (Skeem and Cooke, 2010) and considering antisociality central to psychopathy with scores continuously distributed, are clearly ongoing subjects for debate, however, what it becomes relatively clear is that the antisocial component of psychopathy is undisputable across various definitions and classifications, but such understanding is not extended to criminal behaviour or criminality, therefore it would be highly inaccurate to say that a definition of psychopathy is implicit a definition of criminality. Hare (2001) strongly suggests that psychopathy cannot conceptually or otherwise simply be equated with criminal behaviour, and its problematic theoretical ground rests with agreeing on exact criteria and conceptual boundaries of psychopathy (Huss, 2014). It is the conclusion of this paper that it is crucial for this type of research and knowledge base to be integrated and reflected upon in a larger framework, that at the very least includes ethics, cross-cultural issues and methodological matters.

References:

American Psychiatric Association. (2013). Diagnostic and statistical manual of mental disorders, 5th edition. Washington, DC. American Psychiatric Press.

American Psychiatric Association. (1994). Diagnostic and statistical manual of mental disorders, 4th edition. Washington, DC. American Psychiatric Press.

American Psychiatric Association. (1968). Diagnostic and statistical manual of mental disorders, 2th edition. Washington, DC. American Psychiatric Press.

Bloningen, D. M., Carlson, S. R., Kruger, R. F., & Patrick, C. J., (2003). A twin study of self-reported psychopathic personality traits. *Personality and Individual Differences*. 35(1). 179-197.

Bloningen, D. M., Hicks, B. M., Krueger, R. F., Patrick, C. J., & Iacono, W. G. (2005). Psychopathic personality traits: heritability and genetic overlap with internalising and externalising psychopathology. *Psychological Medicine*. 35(5). 637-648.

Cleckley, H. M. (1947/1988). The Mask of Sanity. Out of print. Retrieved online at http://www.cassiopaea.com/cassiopaea/cleckley-mos.htm

Hare, R. D., & Neumann, C. S. (2005). Structural models of psychopathy. *Current Psychiatry Reports*, 7(1), 57-64.

Hare, R. D., Neumann, C. S. (2009). Psychopathy: assessment and forensic implications. *The Canadian Journal of Psychiatry*. Vol. 54 (12). 791- 802.

Hare, R. D., Neumann, C. S. (2010). The Role of Antisociality in the Psychopathy Construct: Comment on Skeem and Cooke (2010). Psychological Assessment. Vol 22 (2), 446-452.

Huss, M. T. (2014). Forensic psychology: research, clinical practice, and applications. Hoboken, NJ: John Wiley & Sons.

Motzkin, J. C., Newman, J. P., Kiehl, K. A., Koenings, M. (2011). Reduced prefrontal connectivity in psychopathy. *The Journal of neuroscience.* 31 (30), 17348 – 17357.

Ogloff, J. R. P. (2006). Psychopathy/antisocial personality disorder conundrum. Journal Compilation. The Royal Australian and New Zealand College of Psychiatrists. Retrieved from: http://anp.sagepub.com/content/40/6-7/519.full.pdf

Pozzulo, J., Bennell, C. & Forth, A. (2013). Forensic Psychology. New Jersey: Pearson Education Inc.

Skeem, J. L., Cooke, D. J., (2010). Is criminal behaviour a central component of psychopathy? Conceptual directions for resolving the debate. *Psychological Assessment.* Vol 22 (2), 433-445.

Skeem, J. L., Polaschek, D. L. L., Patrick, C. J., & Lilenfeld, S. O. (2011). Psychopathic personality: bridging the gap between scientific evidence and public policy. *Psychological Science in the Public Interest,* 12, 95-162. Available online at
http://psi.sagepub.com/content/12/3/95.full?ijkey=JZXNgVmoiiDLI&keytype=ref&siteid=sppsi

World Health Organisation (1990). International Classification of diseases and related health problems, 10th edition. Geneva: World Health Organisation.

Chapter 10: Conclusion

<u>*"There is a bounty on my head!"*</u>

In mid-January 2022, I came across a public notice about myself available on line and digitally published. It was an ejected uncalculated attack against me from the British Association of Counselling and Psychotherapy (BACP) British Association for Counselling and Psychotherapy (bacp.co.uk) www.bacp.co.uk; it reads like this:

BACP withdrawal of membership notice for Madalina Day, *reference no 00764707. ... December 2021:* Madalina Day, *Reference No 00764707, Registrant ID 221504.*

At that time and by that point, I was no longer a member of the BACP since May 2021; clear correspondence exists, where I invoiced the BACP for continuing contact with me in spite of I legally and clearly terminating all relationships with the association based on the BACP's violence against me including discrimination and harassment for several months involving previous honorary contract that I had with the Croydon Health Services, an NHS Trust. The allegations from the NHS Trust, copied and pasted by the BACP in their notice, are grave, slander and defamatory statements, but also criminal in its essence from both parties: the NHS and the BACP. Nothing suggested in published notice of conduct is actual factual and evidence, all alleged are, in fact, criminal manifestations of a liable NHS Trust for its incompetence, mishandling their records, and gross harassment and discrimination that I have been subjected to by the very NHS Trust that put forward the allegations, and ultimately by the BACP. I worked at the NHS Trust between 2014/ 2021 and year of 2021 or previous years at no point in time included a year 2 or a year 3 of my professional development as the allegations from the BACP stipulate amongst other paradoxes and profanities. The alleged years aspect of the BACP's notice and implicitly the NHS' vexing and liable communication, are very easily and clearly dismantled by my author Alumni webpage part of Birkbeck, University of London; here: Alumni authors — Birkbeck, University of London (bbk.ac.uk) where one of my poetry books is listed:

POETRY

- ### Trials of Poetry Translated: Incercari Poetice, Madalina Day (Psychodynamic Counselling and Cognitive Behavioural Therapy, **2016**)

So, 2016 is my graduation year with final year being 2015/2016 - that is first evidence of slander and defamation with criminal intent from both the BACP and the NHS Trust against me and my professional status. Birkbeck also listed my ***Strategies and self-help from counselling and psychotherapy*** one of my textbooks published in August 2021. In 2016, I had completed my 4th or rather 5th degree (4th final year), and in 2021 I was not studying any degrees other than completing the PhD which had nothing to do with the BACP, the NHS or its staff. My PhD was not mentioned anywhere, and certainly I was not involved with neither organisation about my work on the PhD at any professional level. The BACP notice alleges year 2 and year 3 of professional study – whereas I started my work at the Trust in final year (4th) 2015/2016 so entire published argument is evidently a criminal act performed by the BACP intended statements of harmful abuse, slander and liable defamatory attacks against me via the BACP from the NHS. The BACP also alleges various other extravagantly stupid and criminal assertions that ironically, at times, itself recognises as non-evidence and/or allegations from the NHS Trust being deliberately untruthful and malicious communications in its entirety. For instance, why I would use the Professional Standards Authority (PSA) Logo on my consultancy being advertised on specific directory i.e. counselling directory? That was the case because it was a requirement and it came on automatically on site. Needless to say that I am still an accredited member of the PSA currently as my University degree was accredited, and not the BACP membership. In 2019, I created my own platform www.newbeginningspage.com and at no time, on my own digital platform, I had mentioned the BACP or had a logo from the PSA or any logo mentioning of other professional organisations that I am an integral part of. I do not even have my degrees and all my credentials listed, never had and never will. Similarly, on second marketing and advertising digital platform that I direct since 2019, www.anewbeginningstherapy.com, again no mentioning of professional affiliations, neither my degrees nor associated credentials and titles, not in the least the BACP or PSA's logos.

The Analyst: *There is a bounty on my head*

BACP's notice is simply   criminal, full on spiteful, vexing, and malicious communications from Emma Ulysses, Iain Dockerty (NHS Trust) and the BACP, all so called organisations that proclaim itself as ethical and viable in their interface with the British public at large. The false allegations against I, brought with such violence and maleficence speak for itself on actual terrorist and criminal at large that individuals Ulysses and Dockerty can be identified as, and as to organisations such as the NHS and the BACP's terrorist nature and criminality it is absolutely undoubted. The NHS as a corporation collects clinical data of all patients even if patients not ever using or registering for services, and under GDPR 2018 there is no real accord with the public, which is criminal and terrorist as it stands. Furthermore, the NHS financial profits in terms of research data collected by selling that data without a real opt in or opt out by the British Public. It is the NHS as a corporation that is in fact in breach of multiple legislative Parliamentary acts on a daily basis and concerning the British Public at large. Anyone that thinks that the NHS by being a service free at point of use, the British Public is not implicitly the Guinee pig in all that involves scientific data and otherwise for the NHS, they better start doing some reflection. It is the NHS that at all times is in breach of confidential data by constantly liaising WITHOUT its PATIENTS CONSENT and using all collected data anonymised or otherwise in all levels of research and scientific programmes including Government statistics. The British Public never had been asked for consent and never will, and all processes in the NHS indicating an opt in opt out is only specific to certain programmes, but not to the overall data that the patients had never and will never be able to protect themselves from and indicate a real opt out option. By having a free NHS, the British Public had sold its soul to the NHS, and all for more like also being murdered, because services received through the NHS are currently on high probability equal to death sentences in terms of the real medical care available. So, all in all, it is not I that had breached ethical guidelines and never will be I, not within an already murderous public service that calls itself national health service or any other service however and whenever that may be the case. But, returning to allegations published in 2021 by the BACP: the BACP also mentions allegation on records and breach of data. Again such statements in itself are an impossibility and somehow self-recognised by the BACP as unevidenced statements on the part of the NHS. Nevertheless, the inference is there: slander, liable, defamatory and criminal assertions from the NHS with the BACP as a tool, violently attacking my professional entity and my character. Some can call it professional assassination, but I just see it for what it is: criminal deliberate act punishable in criminal law and in human rights legislation with perpetrators the NHS and the BACP and I targeted and victim. The individuals at the NHS Trust, Emma Ulysses and Iain Dockerty, and the BACP criminality is undoubted to its evidence. It is a fact not an alleged statement. Furthermore, the BACP should cease to exist because it is nothing other than a terrorist organisation that proves itself terrorist in its entire presentation. And to be clear, all analysts are required by law to keep their own records and notes of sessions, but that does not involve GDPR 2018 data and/or personal details of individual NHS staff. The vile and violent action on part of both the BACP and the NHS Trust are failed attempts to discredit me professionally, probably also as a repercussion to my standing up to the NHS Trust Occupational Health Head Iain Dockerty and pointing out his lack of professionalism and criminal attitude towards me and the NHS staff. But this textbook and potentially many other effects of such a violence and criminality, are not going to go adrift and remain within a published space of conduct notice. I am certain that both the NHS and the BACP will suffer enormous and severe consequences of their actions against me for years to come, if not decades – I am hoping that both the NHS and the BACP will cease to exist within next couple of years, mostly for its own sake. Why am I wishing that? Precisely for the protection of British public at large, that being my only goal and aim in all my clinical work.

Why I am certain on such drastic consequences? Here are two aspects.

The first aspect is that the NHS cannot self-sustain itself in any order and absolutely the patching that took place in the last decades is only harming the British public. On the BACP, I do not have much thought nor worry. It is quite evidently clear to me that the BACP is in effect a PONZI scheme, and with all PONZI schemes comes a time of dying one way or another – it is just a question as to when, not if. Second aspect related to the NHS as to why is going to cease to exist shortly, is related to its own attitude of killing itself from the inside, and statistics do not lie. Brexit was the last straw, now is the after war effect where the NHS is just collecting bodies and making more corpses along the way through its malpractice and unsafe services. Am I worried? No, not so much anymore, because it is an irreversible process at this point. Can anyone or anything stop this process? Highly unlikely. Both the NHS and the BACP had fallen on their own swords, so to speak. Now it is just a matter as to when the NHS's final act of breaking into pieces is going to take place.

I will be watching carefully, dutifully, and I shall applaud it when the NHS is changing its name/ faded logo. That is all that I can promise thus far: I will keep an eye for the NHS's logo to disappear. And only after, I shall reclassify my books also as a history category, a history as to how the NHS died by suicide.

THE END